Kaleidoscope of
FARM TRACTORS

By
Nick Baldwin

An MHB Book
Frederick Warne

THE AUTHOR

Like many others from a farming background, Nick Baldwin first learned to drive on the ubiquitous Fordson Model N. He soon progressed to another Ford tractor, this time converted from a Muir-Hill dumptruck that had a splendid turn of speed on the back lanes of Sussex (or so it seemed to a speed-crazy 14-year-old!)

After leaving school, he was apprenticed at the Rover Co Ltd, spending considerable time with the Land-Rover, both in Britain and in service overseas. He then changed horses and went into publishing and after various jobs with transport magazines became Editor of Old Motor Magazine in 1975, by which time he had rescued several early tractors.

He has chosen over 150 photographs to help illustrate some of the varied makes and design trends of the first 60 years of farm tractors and dedicates this book to the enthusiasts who have managed to preserve examples of so many of the models shown. The photographs are not of preserved tractors, simply because Nick Baldwin feels that period views give a more balanced impression of history. In this book they also give a fascinating insight into the British countryside of long ago and farming methods that are all but forgotten.

Nick Baldwin has also produced a book on present-day worldwide tractors for Frederick Warne (Publishers) Ltd (*Farm Tractors*, Warne's Transport Library).

FOREWORD

Tractors have a fascinating history which is virtually concurrent with that of the motor car. The car appeared in Germany in 1886, the tractor in the USA in 1889, both of them rendered possible by Dr Otto and Eugen Langen's production of the 'Otto Silent' 4 stroke i.c. engine in 1876.

The tractor, however, took much longer to attract buyers than did the car, and it was not until the years of the Great War, 1914-1918, that it became at all popular. Then, to a great extent, it owed its success to that famous 'populariser' Henry Ford who, repeating his feat with 'The Universal Car', the illustrious Model T, produced the Fordson Model F tractor, which was destined not only to be produced in larger numbers than any tractor before or since but, due to Ford's price policy in aggressive salesmanship, introduced tractors to farmers the world over.

The depressed state of farming between the two wars did nothing to stimulate demand, but development proceeded, if not apace, gradually and, in most cases, sensibly. The introduction of the practical pneumatic tractor tyre in 1932, and the advent of Harry Ferguson's 'system' of hydraulic control of implements in 1936, accompanied by a steady trend to the adoption of diesel engines, laid the groundwork for the tremendous upsurge in tractor usage and demand which took place during and after World War II. In other words, the farmer, as soon as he could afford to abandon horse power, was, at last, willing and eager to use brake horsepower.

The day of the tractor had come and, in developed countries, the draught animal was soon a rarity to be stared at in exhibitions and 'country fayre' type entertainments.

This book shows the phases of major development with some sidetracks into the fatuous, futile and downright farcical designs of the past. However, the mainstream kept steadily on, now quicker, now slower, but inexorably to the point arrived at today, where the tractor is the 'universal tool' of the farmer, and also the basis of the majority of earthmoving equipment.

Diggers, bulldozers, dumpers and many more all owe their origin to the 'agricultural tractor'. Truly a 'universal tool'.

Charles L Cawood

PREFACE

In this book some fifty years of tractor design from the earliest days is illustrated and described. Though the development is covered as it affected British farmers, it inevitably includes an enormous number of American machines as these greatly influenced British design and were indeed bought in large numbers in this country. Wherever possible I have quoted the power of the individual tractors in the recognised manner, using the two drawbar/belt horsepower figures (eg, International 10/20hp) to make comparisons between models possible. Unfortunately, on occasions this has not been possible as several British manufacturers quoted only RAC formula horsepower based solely on cylinder bore dimensions, whilst American manufacturers from the

thirties tended to express the capabilities of their tractors in terms of ploughing capacity (eg, a three plough tractor), especially if they had not been given a formal rating in a University of Nebraska Agricultural Engineering Dept Test.

Also in describing tractors I have endeavoured to give the lifespan of each model's production, and it is worth remembering that the announcement date quoted for many of the American tractors will be often a year or two earlier than the date at which they first appeared in Britain.

I am greatly indebted for all the help given me in preparing this book to Mr Charles Cawood of Yorkshire and Mr Robert Crawford of Lincolnshire. Both have spent their working lives with agricultural machinery and have remarkable detailed knowledge of just about every conceivable tractor. Both have enormous collections of period tractor litera-

ture which I have been allowed to study and Robert Crawford has one of the largest collections of preserved tractors in the country.

I am also most grateful to Frank Townshend in Sussex, John S Creasey at the University of Reading Museum of English Rural Life for giving me access to their remarkable collection of early farming photographs and to Old Motor Magazine, whose archives have proved invaluable. My thanks also to Nick Georgano, The National Motor Museum, and the various tractor manufacturers for all their help, particularly Massey-Ferguson, International Harvester, Leyland and John Deere.

One of the most significant early designs was the American made Wallis Cub, because it was the first frameless tractor. Here one draws a Ransomes plough in Britain during the early years of the Great War

THE PIONEER YEARS

Mechanical ploughing with steam winching tackle was in use in Britain from the mid nineteenth century, but only the very largest estates or contractors could afford to own their own set.
From the earliest days of mechanically propelled transport, attempts had been made to replace the horse on farm land as well as the roads, but in Britain this met with little success as most farms were too small to bear the cost of their own tractor. An additional complication was that pioneer tractors were usually based on steam traction engines which were far too heavy and cumbersome to work previously horsedrawn implements and stood the risk of sinking or damaging the land.

1   The first form of mechanised ploughing in which the plough was winched from side to side of the field by steam engine was gradually ousted by direct ploughing tractors. However, steam tackle continued in commercial use until the sixties and even enjoyed a brief resurgence during the Second World War, when this photograph was taken. It shows a Fowler breaking a 40 acre field at Chenies, Bucks. Other traditional methods are shown in the background, with a horse gin working an elevator

The first truly British tractors, or agrimotors, as they were called, were the Petter, probably in 1893, and the Saunderson, Ivel and Ransomes machines of 1902. None was a significant sales success, due to lack of capital and apathy, and their makers soon concentrated on other products or went out of business.

Early tractors simply towed their implements and often required both a driver and a machine operator, though from 1904, when the Sharp tractors had a built-in hay cutter, there was a gradual tendency towards mounted implements, notably on the Ideal tractor of 1910, which had a winch for raising its plough. Power take-offs for powering towed machinery, as opposed to simple belt pulleys for static use, did

not appear generally until after the 1914-18 War. However, such machines as the 1913 Lanz had a permanently mounted engine driven cultivator and the 4x4 Maudslay engined Darby-Maskell of 1913 had a mechanically operated rotary plough.

Several stationary engine makers offered farm tractors in the early years, including Petter and Hornsby (who exhibited their first hot bulb oil engined traction engine at the 1896 Smithfield Show and converted it to crawler tracks in 1905). The steam traction engine makers built special lightweight versions of their machines for direct ploughing without much success and most, like Fowler (from 1911), Clayton & Shuttleworth (1911), Marshall (1907) and Foster

(1912) offered petrol/paraffin tractors. These were widely used in the Colonies but once more were too large and expensive for British farms. To obtain traction equivalent to a heavy horse, Saunderson were pioneers in offering all wheel drive tractors in 1906. Indeed, their 3x3 Universal 50hp tractor could successfully plough with a massive Fowler balance plough from a steam winching set. Another way to increase traction was to fit crawler tracks as developed simultaneously in 1904 by Hornsby in Britain and Holt in America. These suited large American farms but did not become commonplace in Britain until more compact tractors appeared in the twenties.

At the first major tractor trials in

2   The First tractors in Britain to be made for direct towing, as opposed to winching implements, were Ransomes in 1849, Twyford/Boydell/Burrell in the 1850's and many more from 1860 onwards, including this Farmers Friend. It was produced in 1878 by Braby of Rudgwick, Sussex, for Mason and

Weyman of Guildford. It was steam powered and was both driven and steered on the single front wheel .

3A and B   Daniel Albone began his tractor experiments in 1897 and produced his first Ivel at Biggleswade in 1902. The Ivel remained in production for some fourteen years with few fundamental changes. This early example had a horizontally opposed twin

cylinder 177 cu ins petrol engine supplied by Aster or, alternatively, Payne and Bates of Coventry, which was mounted longitudinally in the frame and developed 18/22hp at 850 rpm. It had a single forward and reverse gear, though later two speeds were offered, as

was a paraffin vapouriser.

With a three furrow plough it was possible to cultivate six acres in nine hours and as it weighed only around 1½ tons it caused minimal damage to the ground

4   This Wallis and Steevens tractor, made in Basingstoke in 1905, is particularly interesting in that it shows an early attempt to apply steam power to direct ploughing. By mounting ploughs at either end of the machine it did not have to turn at the headlands and was, of course, very similar to the one-way ploughs more normally winched between a pair of ploughing engines. Unfortunately, high weight and lack of adhesion in wet weather limited the effectiveness of the outfit, though it was an idea that was frequently revived in later years - one of the most ingenious being the twin petrol engined four wheel drive French Brabant in 1914

Britain in 1910, staged by the RASE, a McLaren steam ploughing engine put up the best overall performance but the organisers had the foresight to see that 'the oil engine will ultimately best suit the farmer's requirements'. The same foresight was not evident in 1908 when an agricultural expert saw one of the first American tractors in Europe, a single cylinder International, and commented 'one cannot consider it

seriously. It is cheaply built in typical American gas-fitting style'.

Steam in agriculture started its gradual decline with the advent of the internal combustion engine, partly explained by a typical Fowler ploughing set in 1912 costing £2300 when a by-no-means-cheap 30hp Daimler tractor and plough could be bought for £514. Admittedly, however, the Fowlers could do half as much work again as the Daimler and had a greater life expectancy. Indeed, many were still earning their keep thirty years later.

Mann had some success with light steam tractors for direct ploughing from 1911, though another well-known name in the commercial vehicle world, Dennis, did less well with their petrol engined tractor and irrigator of 1909. It was a time when designs of all sorts were tried, but few made the grade, and it was left to the Great War to prove the worth of agricultural tractors in Britain.

4A   Though not to become more than a twinkle in Henry Ford's eye for another ten years, the fact that he was actively investigating power farming is shown by this experimental model with its creator at the wheel in 1907

5 The Dennis agricultural and irrigation motor of 1909 was an ingenious attempt to break into the tractor market by the respected commercial vehicle makers, Dennis Bros of Guildford. It was based on their 28hp fire engine and two ton goods chassis, and was fitted with a 250 gpm Gwynne pump. It was claimed to be capable of towing a two furrow plough in heavy land to a depth of 10 inches

6 A vast steam tractor, built by the Holt Manufacturing Company, the forerunner of Caterpillar tractors. To stop its enormous weight from panning the soil, or from causing it to bog down, the machine was fitted with greeper tracks.. These tracks had been developed independently in 1904 by both Holt and Richard Hornsby and Sons Ltd in England, where they were fitted to a Hornsby oil engined 20hp tractor in 1905. They were extremely successful but created very little agricultural interest in Britain on account of their expense. In 1914 the Hornsby patent rights were sold to Holt for £4000

7 Marshall spent two years in perfecting their 30hp oil tractor before introducing it at the 1908 Smithfield Show. Its two cylinder 850 rpm engine started on petrol and could then be run on vapourising paraffin, and it had three forward speeds, giving up to 6 mph. The device at the front was a cooling tower in which the water cascaded down metal shelves, which were kept cool by the draught created by the exhaust gases. The machine was invented by H W Bamber of London, who claimed that it could do everything that an 8 nhp traction engine could, as well as being light enough for direct ploughing. In a 24 hour trial in 1907 one managed to plough 21½ acres of stubble to a depth of six inches on 2 gallons of petrol and 44 gallons of paraffin. It also achieved considerable success against such opposition as Case, Avery, International, Gaar-Scott and Rumely at the Brandon and Winnipeg Tractor Trials of 1909

8 The Coney was typical of the light tractors available in 1909 and was made by Harrison and Coney of Horsham, who had tested it for three years and were anxious to find a firm willing to produce it in quantity. It used a 15hp three cylinder car engine. Like its contemporaries, it did not use a conventional radiator, but instead had its block connected to a large tank of water, which also acted as ballast

9 Direct motor ploughing was common practice in Canada and the Pacific Coast, South West and North West States of America by 1910. The large size of the farms [the average in Minnesota and Dakota was 825 acres, of which 510 were cultivated annually] made tractors a far more attractive financial proposition than in Britain. Here, three kerosene engined and oil cooled Rumely OilPull tractors plough 50 furrows in one pass on the Canadian Prairies in 1912.

Though made in Indiana, OilPulls were popular in Canada following several successful appearances at the Winnipeg tractor trials. Their makers bought the famous Gaar-Scott traction engine firm in 1912 and were themselves eventually acquired by Allis-Chalmers in 1931

10 The Ideal was an advanced tractor for 1910 in that it had mounted implements raised by winch for one man operation and was laid out in the universally adopted manner of the twenties. It had a 24hp four cylinder Aster engine and a two speed and reverse gearbox and weighed a relatively modest 58 cwt. Its front wheels were offset for ploughing to allow one to run in the last furrow and yet keep both driving wheels on terra firma. The manufacturers lasted for some ten years in Kingston-Upon-Thames and finally Wembley

11 When internal combustion engined tractors started to interest established steam vehicle makers, their machines usually showed their steam origins. However, in the case of the 1911 Clayton and Shuttleworth, a complete break with tradition was made and a 90hp four cylinder petrol/paraffin engine was mounted behind a conventional radiator and under a sheet metal bonnet. The tractor was claimed to be able to pull a 21 furrow plough, but its enormous size and weight of 12 tons restricted its use to the Canadian Prairies and to South America

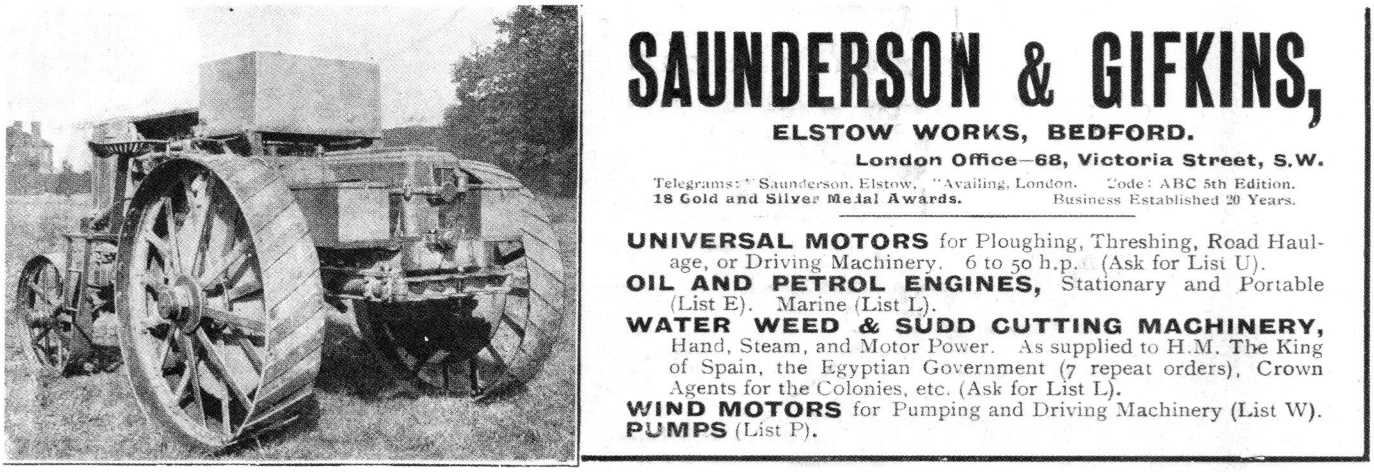

12   When this 30hp machine was made in 1911, the pioneer tractor firm of Saunderson of Bedford were producing 7hp air cooled single cylinder, 14/16hp twin cylinder water cooled and 30 and 50hp four cylinder water cooled engine tractors. They were also well-known for their stationary engines and for wind wheels, pumps and weed cutting barges

13   In 1911 the respected firm of Daimler of Coventry produced their first agricultural tractors. They were a massive 100hp six cylinder Knight sleeve-valve engined machine primarily for overseas use with ploughs of up to 21 furrows and the more practical 30hp machine illustrated here. It had a four cylinder sleeve valve engine, also used in the firm's new three ton truck, and a three forward speed gearbox, giving up to 7 mph. Unlike the larger tractor, which looked like a steam traction engine and initially had its engine mounted in the tender, the 30hp machine had a conventional front mounted engine. These Daimlers were amongst the first tractors of their type to have high speed automotive engines capable of over 1000 rpm as opposed to the slogging oil engines with massive flywheels which were typical of the time

14   A Holt petrol engined tractor of about 1912, built at the company's new Peoria factory, which was to be the home of Caterpillar Tractors in 1925. These were widely used in Britain during the 1914-18 War and ironically some 443 were built in Lincoln by Ruston, Proctor and Co, who in 1918 were to merge with Richard Hornsby, the British crawler track pioneers. The Holt tractors assembled in Britain were identical to the American original shown, except that a single steered front wheel was normally fitted [this was also true of most of the USA versions] and a Peterborough-built 60hp four cylinder Baker-Perkins petrol engine was substituted for the American Buffalo 45hp engine. This engine had a reputation for being able to breathe in any amount of dust without apparent mishap

15A & 15B   This 1911 Koenig St Georges from France was claimed to be equally suitable for load carrying as for cultivation. The 'grubbing drum' driven by chain from the rear wheels could be adjusted for height from the driving seat. Alternative drums for such duties as hay tossing could also be supplied

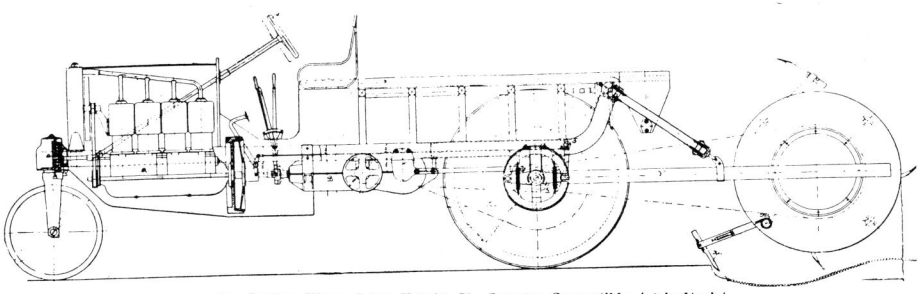

2.—Section View of the Kœnig St. Georges Convertible Agriculturist.

THE GREAT EXPANSION

Many mighty complex and sophisticated mechanised implements were entering production in Europe when the Great War intervened. The forerunner of the Gyrotiller, the Darby-Maskell, has already been mentioned and in addition there were several French designs of rotary cultivator. Then there were the enormous Stock two wheeled six furrow motor ploughs from Germany of which almost 1000 had been sold by the outbreak of war, and the ingenious Brabant. This was a French four wheel drive tractor, looking remarkably similar to today's Muir-Hill except that it had twin engines and simply drove backwards and forwards across the field with a 7-furrow plough mounted at each end of it, which was mechanically raised or lowered depending on the direction of travel.

The outbreak of war seriously restricted British and Continental tractor makers at a time when an enormous expansion in home food production was needed to safeguard the country from the blockade of perishable goods at sea.

None of the existing British tractor firms had any hope of expanding production to cater for the tens of thousands of tractors required to cultivate extra acreage and make up for the loss of manpower on the land. Demand had been so low before the war that few firms were making more

16   The Wallis Cub was the world's first unit built tractor when it appeared in 1913. The 26/44hp Great War example shown was made by the J I Case Plow Works of Racine, Wisconsin, which was finally taken over by Massey-Harris in 1928. The J I Case Threshing Machine Co and Case Plow Co were run by rival branches of the same family, the former [makers of Case tractors] changing its name to J I Case Co in 1928 and acquiring Emerson-Brantingham.

The unit construction of the Cub consisted of the crankcase, transmission case and axle mountings being rolled in one section from steel boiler plate than fifty tractors per year and were completely unable to meet the vast new requirements. As a result, orders were placed with many of America's 100-plus manufacturers who had built up far higher levels of production, thanks to a more receptive home market, caused to a great extent by larger and more affluent farms.

Best known of the imports were the International Titan and Mogul, the Fordson and the Waterloo Boy/Overtime of which many thousands were supplied, but dozens of other makes appeared from dozens of new transatlantic manufacturers.

The Ministry of Munitions asked Henry Ford to provide all necessary drawings and details of his new Fordson so that production could be started in Britain by the British Government. Ford sent Charles Sorenson and his staff to Britain to assist in starting production, and just as all the component contracts were finalised Gotha bombing raids caused a re-think by the Ministry

and the tractor was imported from America instead - over 6000 arriving before the end of the war. The Fordson was one of a new breed of tractor of a shape largely unchanged to this day. The first was the Wallis of 1913 which was made as one unit with the lower halves of the engine, transmission and back axle forming the frame. It had exposed final drive through pinions and ring gears, whilst the Wallis Cub Junior was the first totally enclosed design.

After the war the primitive 'stationary engine on wheels' type of tractor was soon ousted by the new breed of frameless machines and the Fordson did an enormous amount to mechanise farming and replace the horse (350,000 tractors were reckoned to replace each 3 million horses). Of the total American production of tractors in 1921, half were Fordsons. Ford had built 100,000 tractors by August 1920 and in 1923 and 1925 that number was being produced annually. The very low price that this output allowed

put most other manufacturers out of business, even General Motors with their Samson tractor being forced to concede in 1922. Indeed, International were compelled to give ploughs with each antiquated Titan they sold to shift stocks when their new enclosed models were imminent, and when the Fordson was reduced from $525 to $395 two days before the 1925 Minneapolis Tractor Show, several of the remaining manufacturers discovered that this was more than they were having to pay for their engines alone from outside suppliers.

17 The International Titan 10/20 was, with the Overtime, the last of the really successful primitive machines with stationary-type engines and girder frames. The Titan family embraced machines of from 20 to 60hp, single to four cylinder engines, and was made from 1910 to 1924 during which time 60,969 left the International Works in Milwaukeee. The 10/20 was introduced in 1914 and with over 3000 shipped to Britain was the most familiar Titan to British farmers. It had two horizontal longitudinally mounted cylinders and was tank cooled. Two forward gears for up to 2.5 mph and one reverse gear were provided

18A An ingenious American motor plough of 1916 was the Cleveland in which the circular cutting blade was actually rotated by the engine. The driving wheel ran the full width of the vehicle. This example was examined by Fowler for possible British manufacture but nothing came of it and Cleveland soon became known in Great Britain for its Cletrac crawlers instead. The Motor Plow, as opposed to the crawler, was designed by Rollin White of the famous White car and commercial vehicle firm

18B The Moline Universal of 1914 followed the acquisition of the Universal Tractor Co of Columbus, Ohio, by the Moline Plow Co. This Model C Motor Plow was imported into Britain from late 1916 by British Empire Motors of South Kensington and had a horizontally opposed twin cylinder 10/12hp engine, a single gear, and pinion and ring drive. It weighed 25 cwts and was one of the first successful multi-purpose farm power units. Its Model D stablemate of 1917 had a four cylinder engine designed by John Willys, the car maker, and featured electric starting, governing and lighting. In 1929 Moline merged with the makers of the Minneapolis tractor and the Minneapolis Steel and Machinery Co [makers of Twin City tractors] to produce Minneapolis-Moline tractors - well-known in Britain during the Second World War

19A & B The Bull Tractor Company of Minneapolis introduced a cheap, lightweight [initially $395 and 3000lbs] machine in 1913. It sold well in the USA and was marketed in Britain as the Whiting-Bull by the Motor Department of the well-known London store, Whiting Ltd, in the Euston Road. The version sold in Britain 1916-23 [though production ended in 1918] was the Big Bull with auxiliary driven nearside wheel and twin cylinder 12/24hp engine able to run on paraffin. Its price in 1922 was reduced from £395 to £150 in an attempt to improve its prospects against the £120 Fordson.

The example shown here dates from around 1917 and has been fitted with a centre mounted plough, adjustable by the driver. The view of the other side of a similar Bull shows its undriven nearside wheel. The three tanks are for kerosene [largest], water [for injection with fuel] and petrol [smallest tank]

There remained a small market for more completely equipped (items such as power take-offs appeared on International) and better quality or special purpose tractors which allowed many of today's household names to survive. Then in the late twenties Ford moved tractor production to Ireland and later to England when it was appreciated that the enormously successful Fordson had, in fact, sometimes been unprofitable to the company.

In Britain the home tractor producers had a difficult struggle against slumps and American competition, and the best mass-production prospects, the Glasgow and Austin, soon disappeared, though the Austin, considerably revised, continued to be made in France until the 1930s.

20 Walsh and Clark made semi-diesel tractors and Victoria Oil Ploughing Engines at Guiseley, Yorkshire, between 1911 and the early twenties. Their early models looked like typical oil engined Colonial tractors but in 1915 they were redesigned along the steam engine lines shown here. The original model had a pair of side by side cylinders with a colossal bore and stroke of 9ins x 12ins, giving 70 bhp at 320 rpm. Its engine worked on the two-stroke cycle, but the horizontally opposed engine on this surviving late example is a four stroke. It was photographed when lying derelict in Sussex in the early sixties

21 The Mann Patent Steam Cart and Wagon Co Ltd introduced an ingenious small steam vehicle in 1898 which was equally suitable for carrying small loads or for towing implements or trailers. The overall conception had changed very little when this tractor was photographed at Malton station in 1918. From 1910 a determined effort was made to interest farmers in its ability to draw a four furrow plough set at 7 inches in heavy land and the two cylinder 25hp agricultural model was listed until the very end of the company's existence in 1928. To give reduced ground pressure, 2ft 4ins wide rear wheels were fitted

22A & B During 1915 to 1918 International Harvester experimented with Motor Cultivators able to accomplish the bulk of farming work with the aid of mounted implements. These were pioneer users of power take-offs [for driving towed or mounted machinery as opposed to belt-driven stationary applications]. P.t.o. was formally introduced by International in 1918 on the 8/16 Junior and was popularised on the 10-20 gear drive Junior and 15-30. The transverse engined version has a Continental 15hp four cylinder motor driving the wheels underneath it vertically through a forward and reverse gearbox. The later Super Power version was an attempt to simplify the device by using generally available tractor components

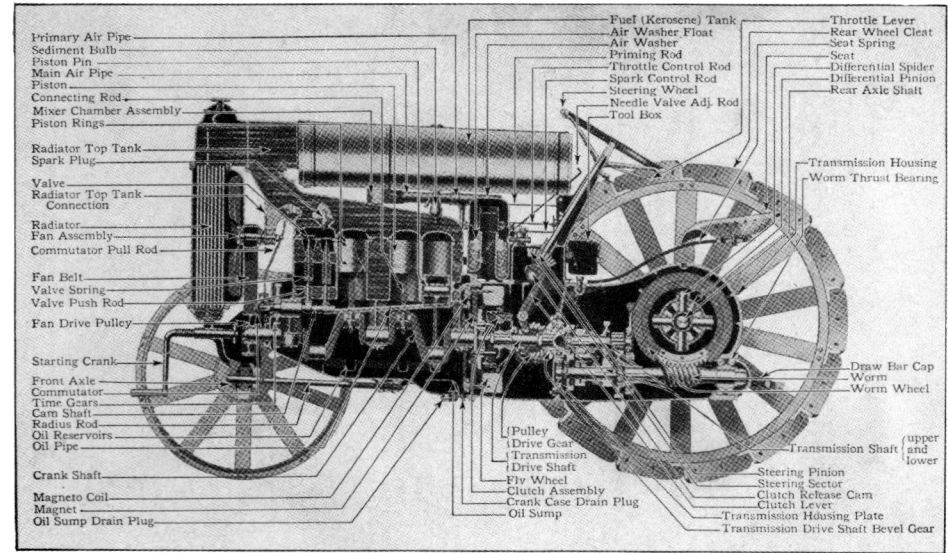

Primary Air Pipe
Sediment Bulb
Piston Pin
Main Air Pipe
Piston
Connecting Rod
Mixer Chamber Assembly
Piston Rings
Radiator Top Tank
Spark Plug
Valve
Radiator Top Tank Connection
Radiator
Fan Assembly
Commutator Pull Rod
Fan Belt
Valve Spring
Valve Push Rod
Fan Drive Pulley
Starting Crank
Front Axle
Commutator
Time Gears
Cam Shaft
Radius Rod
Oil Reservoirs
Oil Pipe
Crank Shaft
Magneto Coil
Magnet
Oil Sump Drain Plug

Fuel (Kerosene) Tank
Air Washer Float
Air Washer
Priming Rod
Throttle Control Rod
Spark Control Rod
Steering Wheel
Needle Valve Adj. Rod
Tool Box

Throttle Lever
Rear Wheel Cleat
Seat Spring
Seat
Differential Spider
Differential Pinion
Rear Axle Shaft

Transmission Housing
Worm Thrust Bearing

Draw Bar Cap
Worm
Worm Wheel

Pulley
Drive Gear
Transmission
Drive Shaft
Fly Wheel
Clutch Assembly
Crank Case Drain Plug
Oil Sump

Transmission Shaft (upper and lower)
Steering Pinion
Steering Sector
Clutch Release Cam
Clutch Lever
Transmission Housing Plate
Transmission Drive Shaft Bevel Gear

23A & B Perhaps the most significant event of all in the early history of tractors was the arrival of the Fordson in 1917. The British Ministry of Munitions were desperate to get a cheap and trouble-free tractor into mass production. Ford was to oblige and British sub-contractors were ready, but the first Gotha bombings so disturbed the Ministry that they encouraged American assembly. 6000 soon arrived in Britain and by 1918, when this example was working in Lincolnshire with an Oliver plough, Ford were producing 25% of all the tractors made in America, a figure which increased to 75% in the early twenties, with 100,000 per year production.

This was the first cast iron unit frame tractor, a system soon universally adopted, and it had a 20-23hp four cylinder engine with underslung worm drive. Lubrication was by splash, and ignition by a low tension flywheel magneto and high tension coils.

Its low weight of 23 cwt reduced both ground pressure and manufacturing costs. The result was that it could be retailed for £120 in 1920/1 and thus reach a wider market than any previous tractor

24A, B & C   Three examples of International Moguls which came in a variety of sizes from 60hp twins to the 8/16hp single cylinder machine most familiar to British farmers after its introduction in 1914. Over 600 were imported, plus a further 350 twin cylinder 12/25s and 177 enlarged 8/16 called 10/20 [these had two speed and reverse gearboxes in place of the single forward and reverse on the 8/16]. The first Mogul was built in 1910, five years after the first International tractor, and by the time production ended in 1919, 20,385 had been produced.

International Harvester was formed in 1902 with the amalgamation of a number of individual implement makers, including Deering and McCormick, and was by far the largest tractor producer before the arrival of the Fordson. Their output of 200 tractors in 1907 had expanded to 3000 in 1912, which gave them over a third of total USA tractor production

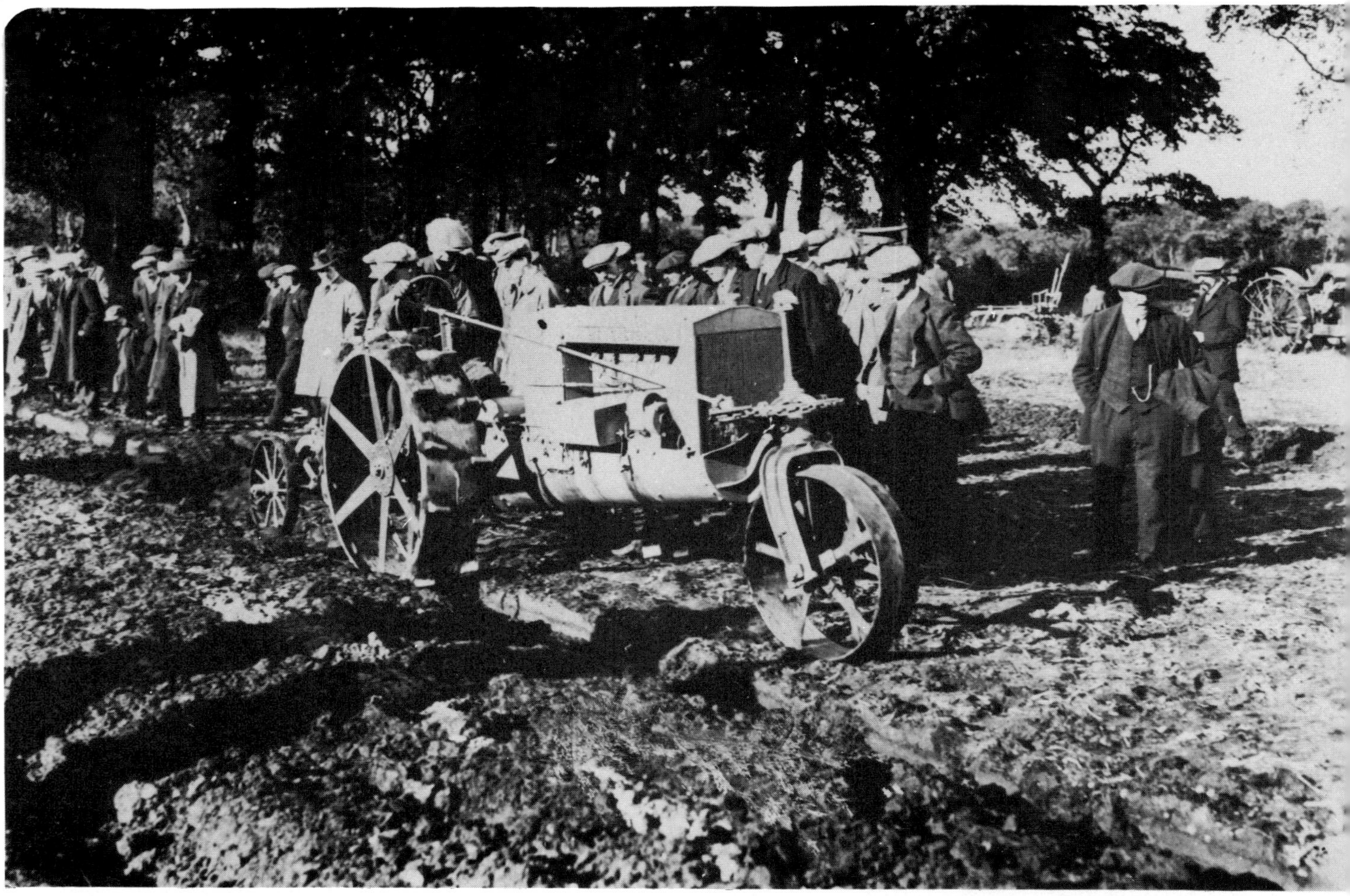

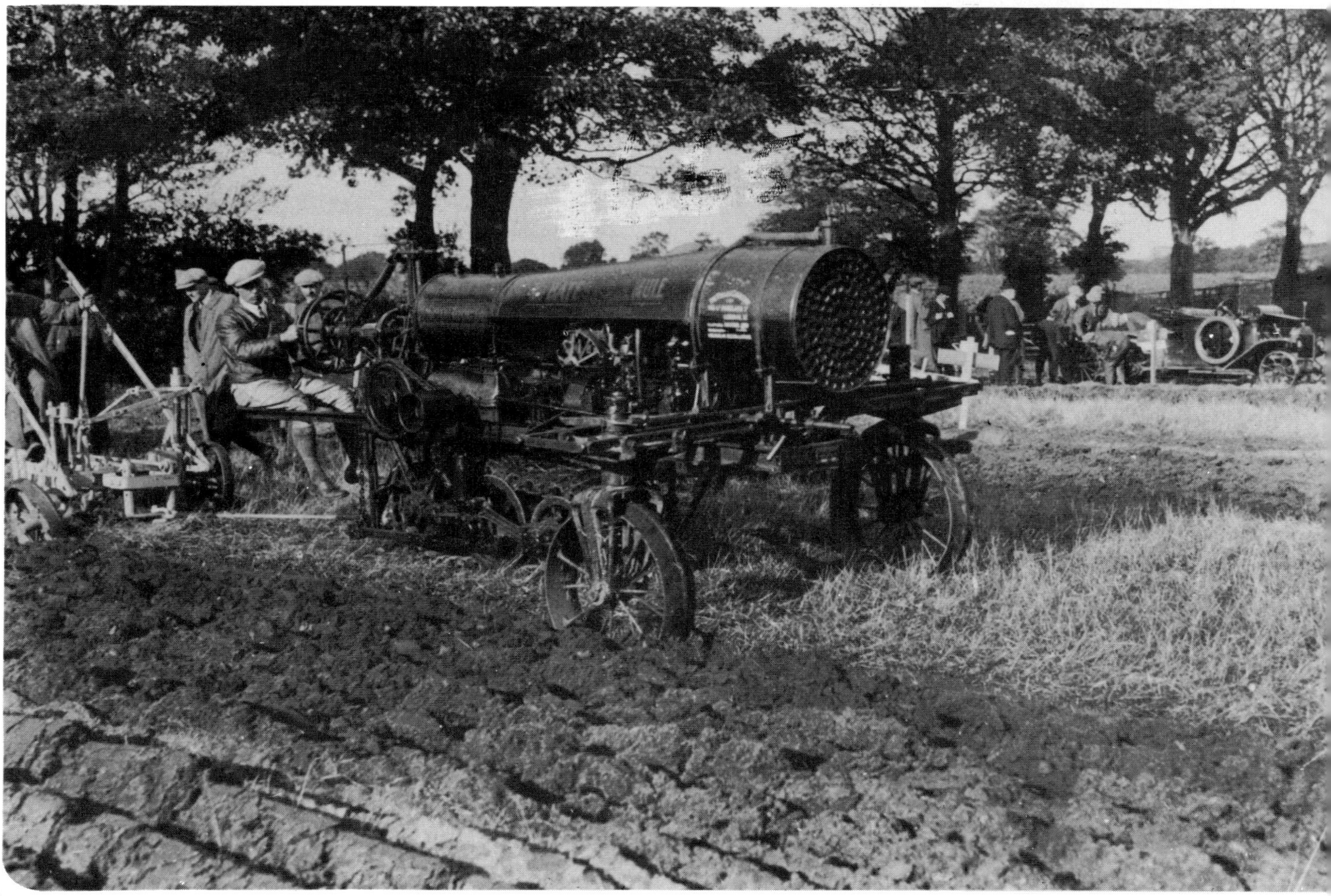

25 [*left*]   Like the bigger Cub, the Wallis Cub Junior was a frameless tractor. It was introduced in 1915 and differed from its larger sister in having a 13/25hp four cylinder paraffin engine and in having enclosed drive to the rear wheels. The Cub had exposed rack gears around its rear wheels ingeniously lubricated by the oil and carbon from two exhaust outlets trained onto them.

The single front wheel of the Cub Junior could be turned at right angles to enable the tractor to turn within the 93 inches of its wheelbase. Note the bear cub to show the driver which way the front wheel is pointing

27   The Interstate 'Plow Man' tractor was marketed in Britain by Austin during the 1914/18 War and afterwards for a short time by the Vulcan Car Agency of Gt Portland Street, London.

It had a single forward gear, pinion and ring drive and the peculiar steering system shown in which one front kingpin was extended upwards to carry the worm and segment. 15/30 and 13/30 horsepower four cylinder versions were available

26 [*left*]   The Bates Steel Mule was intended to take the place of draught animals and be controlled from the implement it was working. It had a four cylinder 20/25hp paraffin engine and in 1916 it cost the equivalent of £180 in America and over 1000 had been sold with production running at the rate of 25 per week.

It was hopelessly top heavy and was imported until about 1918 by Austin and then Vulcan, after which it developed into a more conventional range with full or half track tractors and was imported until 1929 by the Mercury Truck and Tractor Co, better known today for their Reliance-Mercury industrial tractors

28 One of the most important tractors to appear during the 1914-18 War was the International Junior or 8-16hp Kerosene Tractor, which was produced from 1917 to 1922 in Chicago. Approximately 33,500 were made, of which around 2500 came to Britain from 1919. Until mid-1919 they had three bearing crankshafts, four cylinder vertical engines [VB model] and afterwards only two bearings [HC and IC models, both of which had large nearside mounted air cleaners]. RAC horsepower rating was 25.6, cylinder liners were renewable, and three forward and one reverse gear were provided together with chain drive and overhead valves. The radiator was housed at the rear of the bonnet to avoid accidental damage.

The example shown is towing a McCormick binder, behind which a patent stooker automatically upended four sheaves at a time

29   Saunderson's principal model from 1916
was the two cylinder [5½x8ins bore and
stroke] 25hp Model G which had a drawbar
pull of 2700 lbs. Here it is seen in the 1919
Lincoln Trials where it ploughed 0.83 acres of
light land per hour at a cost of 5/3d per acre
in fuel. A more streamlined Light-Weight
20hp model was also offered until 1925 and
thereafter only the G was listed until the last
was sold in the early thirties. From 1925 the
tractors were usually known as Crossleys
following their company's takeover by the
Crossley Bros of stationary engine fame

30   The 1919 Pick from Stamford was a
one-off design which featured a 30hp four
cylinder engine mounted transversely,
powering a full width driving roller. The
intricacies of its nine speed transmission were
not elaborated upon and it was presumably
either a single speed machine with nine
throttle settings or else had variable friction
drive. When the tractor reappeared the
following year, it had taken on a more
conventional appearance and had four wheels.
It was listed until 1924

31 A well-liked First World War machine was the Waterloo Boy, known in Britain as the Overtime Model N. The original LA model had first appeared from the Waterloo Gasoline Engine Co of Iowa in 1912 and production had built up from 12 in the first year to 8000 in 1918, the year in which the company was acquired by John Deere. Production continued until 1923, when the first John Deere tractor appeared. The Model N had a two cylinder 12/25hp engine and a two forward speed and reverse gearbox

32 The 1919 Weeks-Dungey New Simplex was a refined version of a compact orchard tractor produced by William Weeks in Maidstone from 1915. It had a Waukesha 30hp four cylinder engine with in-unit 3 forward and reverse gearbox and pinion and ring drive which, by 1919, was totally enclosed to reduce wear. Another change had been the replacement of the original side-mounted cooling tank by a conventional radiator. Tractors were discontinued in 1925, though other farm machinery was made until ten years ago

33 The Glasgow was the result of a major attempt to mass produce tractors in Britain. D L Motors, John Wallace and Sons Ltd and Carmuirs Iron Foundry combined and bought the Government's 12 acre National Projectile factory at Cardonald in 1919. 5000 tractors per year were planned from a workforce of 2000-3000 employed on a profit sharing basis. The first five years' production was sold in advance to the British Motor Trading Corporation, who promptly ran into financial difficulties [they were also involved with the mass-produced Bean car]. Few Glasgows followed D L Motors' original 1918 prototypes but they were, nevertheless, most interesting technically. The 27hp Waukesha engine [a few had Burt-McCollum sleeve valve engines] drove all three wheels via a two speed forward and one reverse speed gearbox. The machine was unit built and there was no differential, the front wheels being compensated for differing speeds on lock by ratchets

34 The Fowler motor plough was used with considerable success in the 1919 Edinburgh Tractor Trials. It was built under Wyles and Fowler Patents, Albert Wyles having introduced a smaller 4hp, single furrow machine in 1912 after two years of experiments in the market gardens around Evesham. This Fowler version had a twin cylinder 14hp engine able to run on petrol or paraffin, although when Fowler first began to make the Wyles machine at Bristol in 1913 it was still single cylindered. The example shown dates from 1917 and is a DC model, towing a self binder, and Fowler soon went on to build versions of up to 50hp before devoting their attention to Gyrotillers and crawler tractors

35 This Gray tractor from Minneapolis was made for about ten years from 1914 and appeared at the 1919 Lincoln Tractor Trials. It had a transversely mounted 36hp [18hp at drawbar] Waukesha four cylinder engine which drove a 54 inch wide roller across the rear of the frame by chains, via a series of straight-cut gears. The mechanism was covered by a sort of corrugated iron shed.

Though later made in Essex, the Maskell motor plough shown here [the machine in the background] was produced by Petters of Yeovil with four cylinder engine of 25.6hp and single forward and reverse gears

36 Martin's Cultivator Co Ltd of Stamford made ingenious tracked motor ploughs from 1915. An early experimental model had a central motor unit with a pivoting plough frame which allowed shares at either end to be lowered. In this way the machine did not have to be turned on headlands and worked more like a winched balance plough. In 1919 the normal one directional plough model was joined by a four wheel tractor which sold in very small quantities until 1923. Both types of machine had Dorman 30hp four cylinder paraffin engines and the wheeled tractor had pinion and ring drive and two forward gears. It cost £450 in 1919

37 The Santler One-Way Motor Plough emanated from Malvern Link in 1919. It had a two cylinder 25hp paraffin engine and two speeds, both forwards and in reverse. As can be seen, it was another attempt to motorise a balance plough and thus avoid turning at the headlands. The driver had a single steering wheel with seats on both sides for use in either direction of travel. Very few of these, or Santler's Morgan-like light cars, were made

38 Emerson-Brantingham built a range of tractors at Rockford, Illinois, and was finally bought out by the J I Case Threshing Machine Co in 1928. Their first British concessionaires were Bentley and Bentley, soon to become famous for their Bentley cars, but at that time looking for a replacement for the French DFP cars they had sold before the war. This example is shown on trial at Edinburgh in 1917. It had a four cylinder 25hp engine and two forward and one reverse gears, giving a top speed of 2.32 mph. In the background is an 11 bhp one cylinder two speed Wyles motor plough

39 The Heider model D tractor of 1919 was rated at 9/16hp and had a four cylinder petrol/paraffin engine. Transmission was by friction discs, giving one to four mph. The tractor was later renamed the Rock Island and in 1937 the Rock Island Plow Co was bought by J I Case. Early sales in Britain were handled by Willys-Overland, of car and truck frame. Heider of Cedar Rapids themselves had made tractors since 1910 and sold out to the Rock Island Plow Co about 1918.

Note the mounted plough and mechanical, though non-hydraulic, lifting gear. A similar system was used by Case until about 1950

40 The Samson Sieve Grip appeared at the Edinburgh Trials in 1919. It had a 12/25hp four cylinder petrol/paraffin engine and twin close-set 18 inch wide driving wheels. It had enclosed single forward and reverse gear transmission and was capable of up to 3½ mph. The Samson Sieve Grip Tractor Co of Stockton, California, was bought by W C Durant of General Motors in 1917 and transferred to Pontiac, Michigan. Despite the introduction of a conventional Ford-type tractor at the end of the war, General Motors were largely unsuccessful in the tractor market and they ceased production in 1922

41 The Denning from America became the GO [General Ordnance Co of New York City who were anxious to replace their lost armaments contracts] in May 1919. The shaft in front of the rear wheel was normally fitted with a belt pulley. The tractor weighed just under two tons and could draw four 14ins plough shares in medium land. It was sold in Britain by the Vulcan Car Agency of Great Portland Street, London, who had acquired several tractor franchises from Austin, when the Birmingham company decided to make its own tractors instead of importing American designs

42 The GO model G tractor evolved from the Denning in 1919 and was made for some three years. It had a 14/27hp Waukesha engine and friction drive, variously described as giving three forward and three reverse speeds or six forward and one reverse. It was extremely expensive at £500, which included £30 worth of essential spares - presumably replacement discs for the friction transmission! The machine incorporated an early example of steering brakes in which each rear brake had a separate control

43 Blackstone and Co of Stamford, later associated with Agricultural and General Engineers and then R A Lister of Dursley, and well-known for their stationary engines, produced Creeper-Track tractors from the end of the Great War to 1925. In 1919 they also offered four wheeled versions of the same machine at the same price of £500. Chief peculiarity of the design was the use of the company's three cylinder 25hp oil engine. This could be started by hand or compressed air and ran on paraffin injected into the combustion chambers and fired by spark. Whereas most other tractors ran on paraffin and required petrol to start them and warm up the induction manifold sufficiently to vaporise the fuel, the Blackstone could cold-start on paraffin because it was injected as mist

44 Britain's answer to the Fordson was the R-model Austin which appeared in 1919. In line with Austin's post-war one model policy it used the engine from their 20hp car and projected 30 cwt lorry, but with a different sump to allow for unit construction. It did well at tractor trials in France and England and in 1919 Austin bought a factory at Liancourt, midway between Calais and Paris, where they planned to produce 2000 per year for the French market. At £360 in 1921 it was three times more expensive than the Fordson and though the price soon dropped to £225 it never enjoyed mass sales. From 1927 all production took place in France [where it was protected by tariff barriers] with occasional imports to Britain. The French versions used three forward speed gearboxes which were only optional on the two speed English version. The young man on the binder is the author's future father-in-law

45 The Clayton tractor from Clayton and
Shuttleworth Ltd of Lincoln was one of the
earliest British compact crawlers and was
produced for some twelve years from 1916 and
in the form shown above from late 1918
onwards. It had two forward gears giving 1900
and 4710 lbs drawbar pull respectively and
was powered by the paraffin version of
Dorman's well-known 4JO 6326cc 40hp
engine which was widely used in trucks during
the Great War and afterwards. Aster engines
were also offered. Note the conventional
steering wheel to operate the track steering
cluthces.

Clayton were acquired by Marshall in the
mid-twenties and were associated with
Hofherr-Schrantz-Clayton and Shuttleworth
of Hungary, whose HSCS Steel Horse tractor
appeared at the World Tractor Trials in 1930,
and was the forerunner of the modern Dutra

46 The American Wallis tractor was
produced in Britain by Ruston and Hornsby
between 1920 and '29. It weighed 39 cwt and
had a four cylinder paraffin engine with
detachable cylinders and cylinder head. It
developed 28 bhp at its normal working speed
of 875 rpm and exerted a 2600 lb drawbar pull
at 2½ mph. Wallis in America was owned by
the J I Case Plow Co, which Massey-Harris
bought in 1928 and thus acquired rights to
make the Wallis tractor. As already explained
in caption 16, it is not to be confused with the
J I Case Threshing Machine Co who made
Case tractors and changed its company name
to J I Case Co in 1928

47 The history of American tractors in Britain is greatly confused by the fact that many were sold under the name of their local agents. Indeed, to some extent the same was true in America with certain makes available under a variety of names. This tractor which appeared at Lincoln in 1919 was called the Moseley, but in fact was an Illinois Super-Drive with 40hp four cylinder engine. It originally had two forward speeds with optional ratios giving four choices, but by 1919 had a conventional three forward speeds and reverse gearbox. The springs on the wheel were designed to absorb sudden shock loadings on the transmission, such as occurred when an obstruction was hit by a plough share

48 Like the Wyles motor plough the Crawley was developed by a farming family. The first prototype was made in 1908 and in 1914 Garrett briefly took on its manufacture, no doubt taking a leaf from the book of their rivals, Fowler. However, only three were made before Crawley established their own factory in Saffron Walden, which carried on until 1924. Early examples had conventional front mounted radiators and four cylinder Buda engines which consumed 15 pints of Taxibus spirit per acre when hauling a three furrow plough.

The tractor in the background is a 14/28hp four cylinder Avery, made in Peoria, Illinois, and sold in Britain by R A Lister & Co Ltd of Dursley, Glos, the well-known engine and implement makers

49 The Kardell Truck and Tractor Co had a brief existence in St Louis, Missouri, and had their British sales in 1920/21 handled by Bramco Ltd of Coventry, who had previously sold the Bates Steel Mule. The Kardell tractor cost £475 and had two forward gears giving 2¼ and 3½ mph plus 2 mph in reverse. Power was provided by a 25hp Mid-West four cylinder engine. The tractor could be adapted to be driven from controls extended over the towed implement. The machine was unit built on similar lines to the Fordson and around 6000 had been made in two years production before it appeared in Britain. Kardell's original Waukesha engined machines had been convertible to 3 ton trucks by adding frame extensions

50 A general view of the 1919 Edinburgh Tractor Trials showing a Straits tractor in the foreground with two converted Ford Model T cars behind and an International Mogul. Several firms offered Ford conversion kits which, it was claimed, allowed the tractor to be used as a car within twenty minutes. The Killen-Strait [as it was usually called in Britain] was an American tractor with four cylinder engine governed to 850 rpm. It had a front track for steering and offset track drive at the rear balanced on the nearside by a single undriven steel wheel. It had single forward and reverse gears and could pull up to five tons or a three furrow plough.

The tracks of the Straits were lozenge-shaped to enable the tractor to extricate itself backwards if its tracks lost traction forwards. A three tracked Straits was the basis of the first tracked armoured fighting vehicle in 1915

51 The Case and Cletrac won first and second prizes respectively in the up to 24 horsepower class in the 1920 Lincoln Tractor Trials. The 15/25hp Cletrac was made by the Cleveland Tractor Co in the USA and sold in Britain by H G Burford, who also marketed American Fremont-Mais trucks under his own name. The Case Threshing Machine Co had been a famous steam traction engine maker which had turned its attention to internal combustion engined machines in 1911 following heavier i.c. tractors from 1892. In 1920 it offered 10/18, 15/27 and 22/40hp models to British farmers. The 15/27 shown here had a four cylinder vertical engine mounted transversely in front of the driving wheels

52 [*Bottom left*] **The famous Birmingham engineering firm of Alldays and Onions made 30hp tractors based on their successful commercial vehicle components in the last two years of the Great War. With a weight of three tons and a price of £630 they were uncompetitive with the post-war American tractors and after appearing in France in 1919 and at the Lincoln Tractor Trials, they were quietly discontinued. Note the unusual spoke construction and the spuds fitted only to the top of the rear wheel in this posed photograph. The tractor was unusual in featuring sprung axles, which could be locked rigid for land work, and for its 100 gallon water ballast tank over the rear wheels**

53A & B [*Right and Below*] **Henry Garner was an enterprising Birmingham garage owner who imported both American trucks and tractors and sold them under his own name. The trucks appeared in 1915 and the Garner tractor in 1918. The tractor was made by Wm Galloway of Waterloo, Iowa, and had a 28.9hp petrol/paraffin engine and three forward speeds giving 1½, 2¾ and 5 mph at 900 rpm governed speed. Cheaper competitive tractors proved too much for the Garner despite such publicity stunts as ploughing 800 acres non-stop and towing a threshing machine from London to Birmingham in 24 hours 4 mins, and it was finally discontinued in 1924**

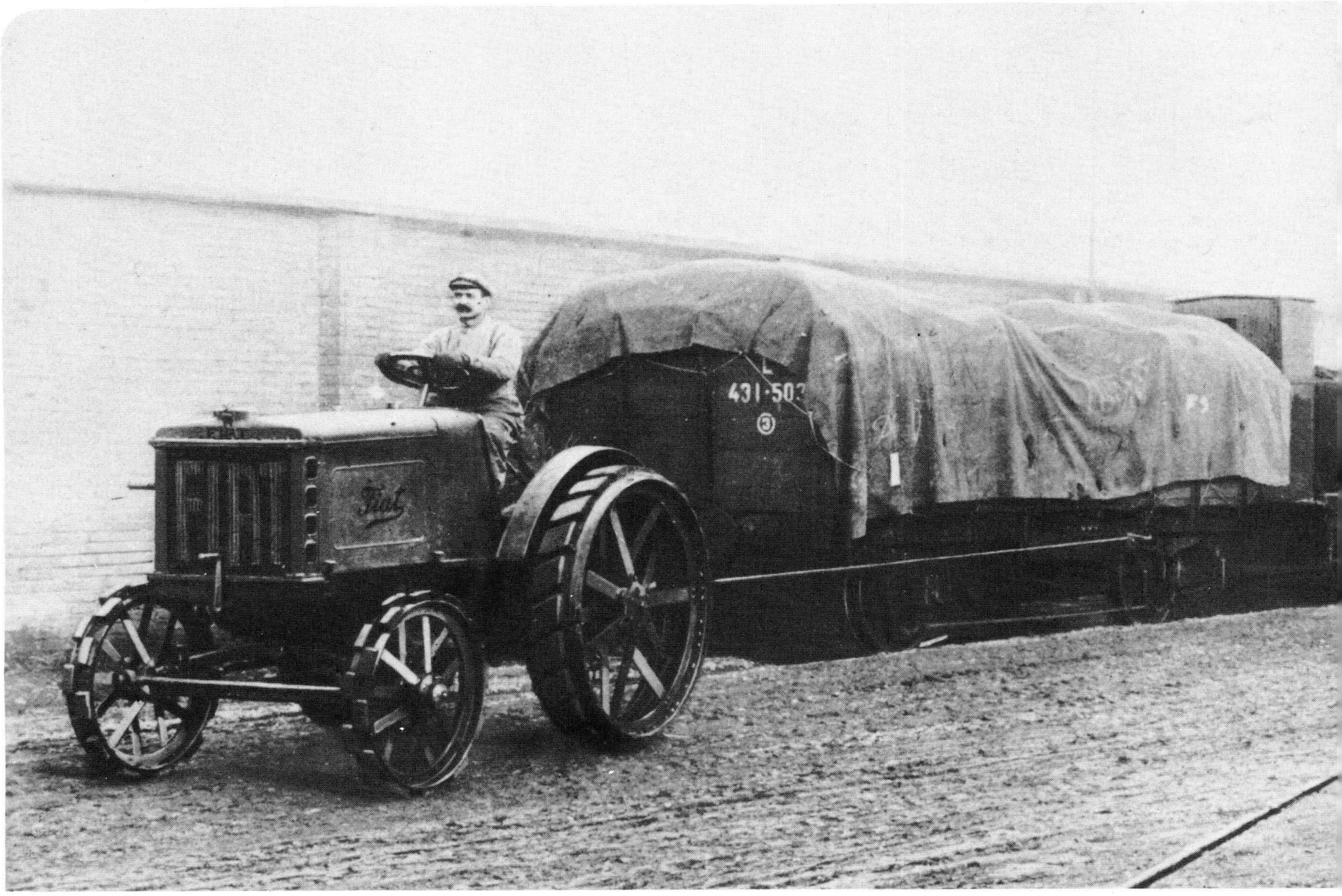
Fiat

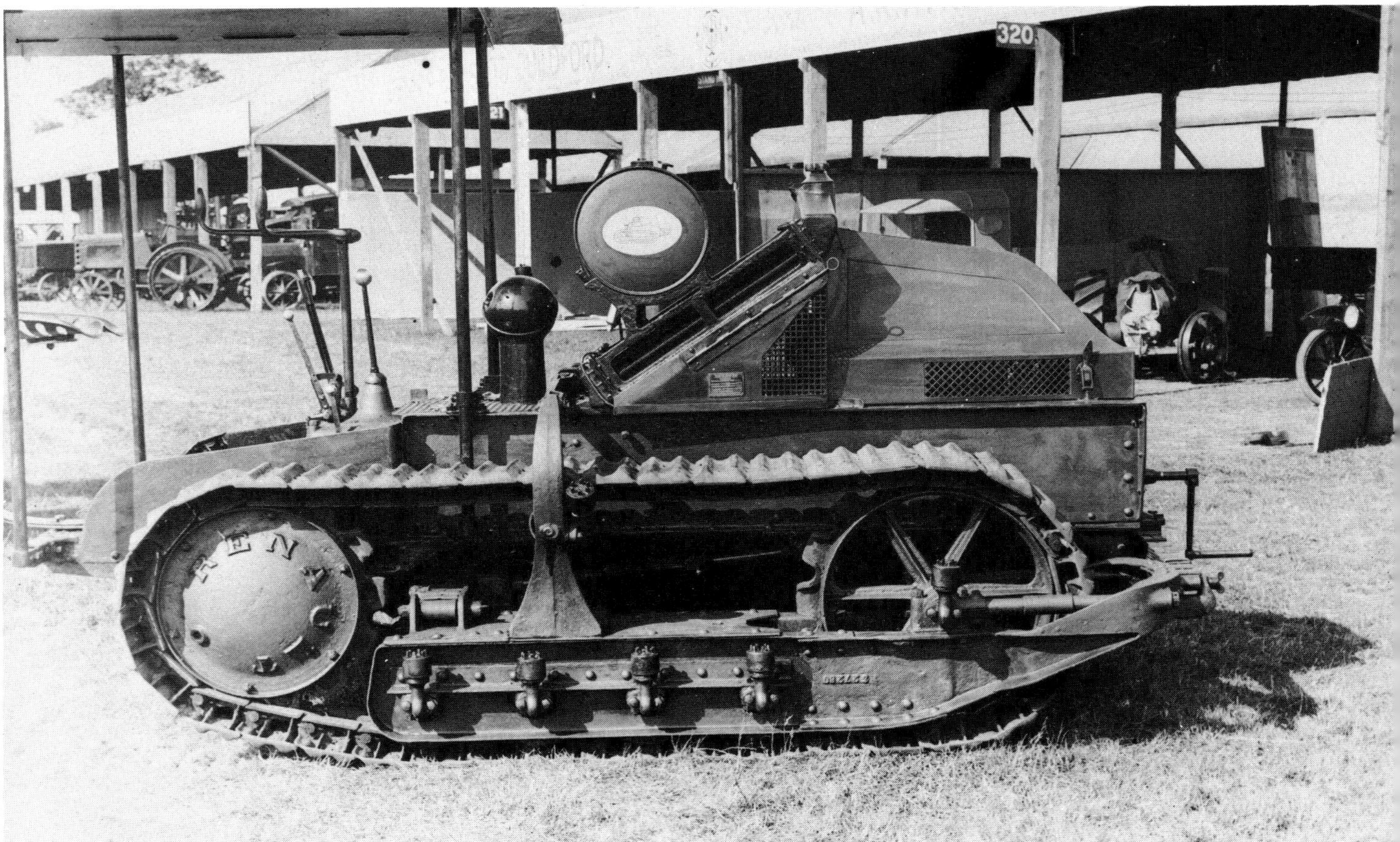
320

54 [Left] Fiat tractors were imported into Britain soon after the Great War and by the end of 1920 the combined 20,000 acre farms of W Dennis and Sons of Lincoln were using no less than 19. The example shown here is a model 702 18/25hp machine demonstrating its tractive effort by moving a 105 ton train. It was regarded as an up-market copy of a Fordson F.

Fiat tractors have been sold intermittently in Britain ever since

55 [Lower left] Renault crawler tractors were offered in Britain for some ten years from 1921. This is the 22.4hp four cylinder HI model exhibited at the Royal Show in 1921. It weighed 3½ tons, had a 3 ton drawbar pull and could draw a six furrow plough with a petrol consumption of 2 gallons per acre. Note Renault's familiar coal scuttle bonnet with rear mounted radiator, in this case mounted at an angle, and the illustration of a Renault tank to show their past experience with crawler tracks on their Great War *char d'assaut*. Wheeled Renault tractors were offered after 1927. In the background is a Fordson minus radiator and several Fiats

56 A K Smith designed his Silent Knight tractor in 1913 in the light of experience with agrimotors in the Colonies. It had a 20hp two cylinder engine and the first batch was produced in Earle's shipbuilding yard at Hull. He then formed a syndicate to produce it in quantity at Hemel Hempstead as the Omnitractor and the firm remained in business until the end of 1921, by which time the manufacturers were Talbot and Davison of Lowestoft. The final models had conventional radiators, as shown here, though earlier ones had a vertical cylinder of tubes as on the contemporary Avery. Ploughing speed was 2¼ mph

57   The Twin City 12/20 paraffin tractor was sold in Britain from 1920 to '29 by Fairbanks Morse, the well-known stationary engine manufacturers, and made by the Minneapolis Steel and Machinery Co [who also made the Bull, though they did not sell it themselves and are not to be confused with the Minneappolis Threshing Machine Co who made the Minneapolis tractor]. Its engine was also used in the company's 3½ ton lorry which, running on petrol, was rated at 30/40hp. An unusual feature of the lorry version of the engine was the use of four overhead valves [2 inlet, 2 exhaust] on each of its four cylinders. The tractor weighed 4200lbs and had a two forward and one reverse speed gearbox. In 1916 Twin City produced the largest tractor of its day, with a 120hp six cylinder kerosene engine for use on the biggest American and Canadian farms

58 The Fordson was produced in America for ten years from 1917 and was briefly assembled in Cork, Ireland, between 1919 and '23 and again in 1929-32. This example of around 1925 was photographed in Kenya. Unlike the original Model F it has enclosed radiator sides and the fourteen in place of twelve spoke steel wheels that were adopted from late 1919. 737,977 were made before American production ended in 1928. In addition 7605 Fs were made in Ireland 1919-23 followed by 31,444 Ns from the Irish factory 1929-32

59 Steam power still held a certain attraction for some farmers brought up with the agricultural traction engine. In America, International Harvester experimented with this paraffin-fired 5300 lbs tractor in 1922. Boiler pressure was up to 600 lbs per square inch and the tractor could pull a three to four furrow plough. Steam tractors for direct ploughing were also offered immediately after the First World War by various firms, including Baker and the Bryan Harvester Co in the USA and by Mann, Garrett and Summerscales in Britain [the latter having a vertical boiler in a tricycle frame and a V-4 25 bhp engine]. Only one was made and only a handful of Garretts

60 The history of all-wheel-drive tractors goes back to the early days of the industry, but was not widely adopted by many farmers or 'big name' tractor makers until taken up by Massey-Harris in 1930, though General Motors' Samson division had made the Iron Horse 4x4 in 1919. Several small firms offered four wheel drive tractors in the USA in the 1920's, notably the Wilson, the Wizard, the Fitch and the Storey Flexible-4-Drive shown here. The Storey was significant to the British scene in that its inventor was responsible for the design of the Fowler Gyrotiller. It was also important for its early use of pivot-steering, now widely used on the largest farm tractors

61 After years of unconventional tractor designs by today's standards, International introduced the unit construction and vertical four cylinder engined 15/30 and 10/20 in 1921 and 1922 respectively. Sold under both the McCormick-Deering and International names, the 10/20 remained in production until 1940, by which time 215,793 had been made. The 15/30, with its built-in power take-off, ballbearing crankshaft, overhead valves and renewable cylinder liners [also features of the 10/20, which it closely resembled] was available as the 22/36 from 1930 and by the end of the model run in 1934 production had amounted to 156,000.

The photograph was taken in the mid-twenties and shows a threshing contractor setting out for work in the Cotswolds on a 15/30

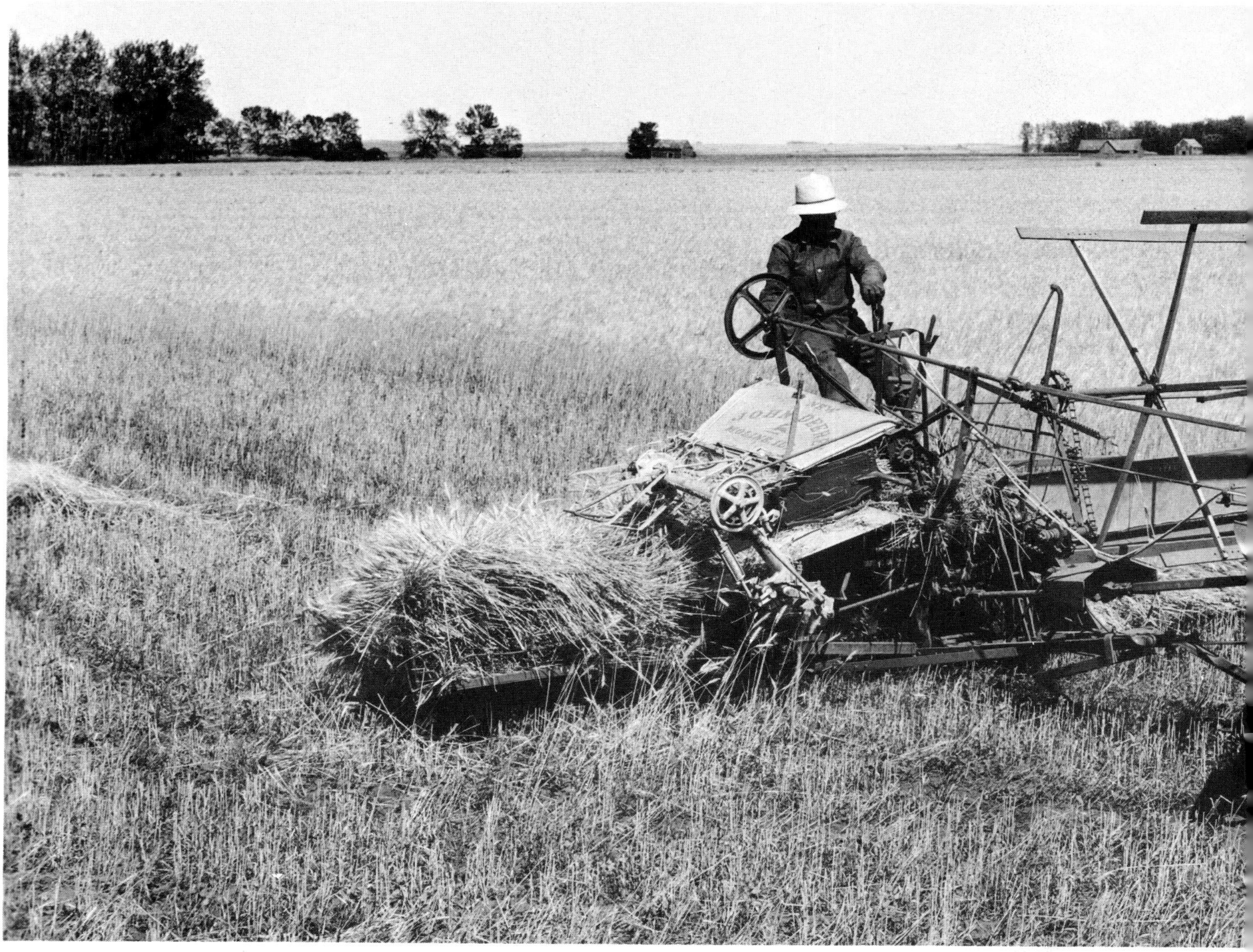

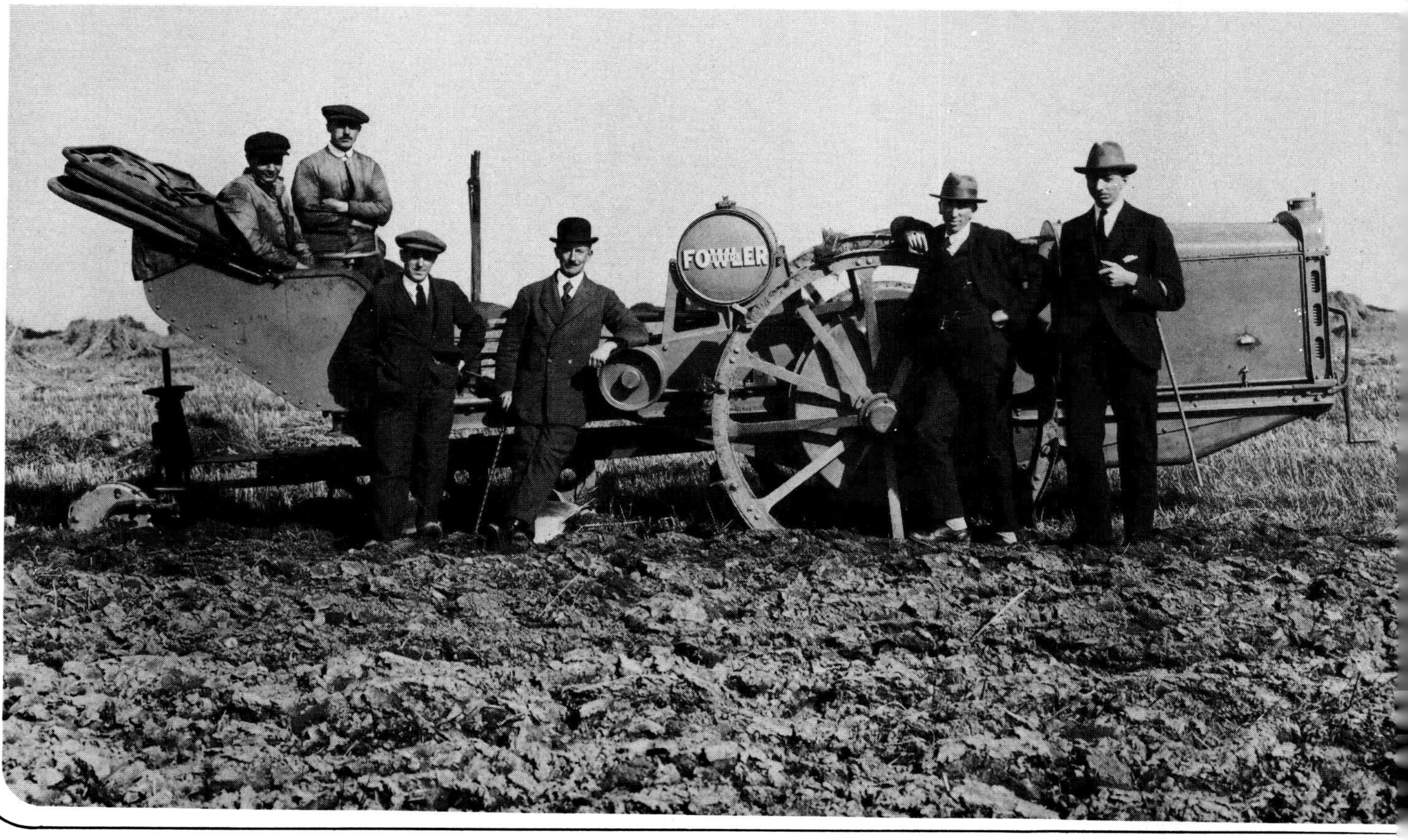
FOWLER

62 After John Deere bought the Waterloo Gasoline Engine Co in 1918 they continued to produce the Waterloo Boy [called Overtime in Britain] with minor modifications such as replacing its chain and barrel steering with stub axle steering, until replacing it with the John Deere Model D in 1923. The Waterloo firm could trace its roots back to 1892 when its founder, John Froelich, built one of the earliest internal combustion engined tractors on record.

The Model D had a conventional tractor shape, though a somewhat unconventional horizontal engine position. Its twin cylinder engine developed 15/27hp. For one-man reaper operation, the tractor's controls could be moved to the implement, as shown here

63A Following their early Wyles motor ploughs, Fowler discontinued two cylinder machines and replaced them with a range of four cylinder ploughs in 1923 with engines of 16 to 50 horsepower, which they produced until 1927. This example appears to be the largest three furrow version, which could exert 6000 lbs tractive effort and run on petrol or paraffin. Following the end of their motor ploughs, Fowler worked on their Gyrotiller and also on their range of crawler tractors, introduced in the early thirties

63B Advertisements of the early '20's had an unfamiliar vagueness about them, as in the case of the Cletrac Junior and Large model. They were, in fact, of 17hp/17 cwt and 25hp/35 cwt respectively

THE LATE TWENTIES AND THIRTIES

Though the tractor shape and constructional methods of today can be traced back to the 1913 Wallis and the Fordson, it was in the thirties that such items as diesel engines, hydraulics and pneumatic tyres were first offered commercially. It also saw the end of countless small tractor manufacturers as the 'big names' took an increasing share of the market. Between 1920 and 1930 four-fifths of the American manufacturers disappeared or were taken over, yet annual production increased by around 200%.

64A The Fowler Gyrotiller was produced at the request of a Mr Storey from America, whose 4x4 tractor was illustrated earlier. He had tried to interest several manufacturers in the USA and Germany, including Caterpillar Tractors. This is the first example of 1927 and the invention was soon vindicated by sales of four in 1929, eight in 1931, forty in 1933 and 106 in 1935. It was developed for sugar cane cultivation in the West Indies and was soon adopted for other heavy agricultural purposes, such as deep cultivating and scrub clearance. Fowler were glad of the opportunity to develop and make the Gyrotiller as it corresponded with the final decline in their steam ploughing engine activities and before their diesel crawler tractors were introduced

64B In the death throes of winch plough manufacture, Fowler made the ingenious Mono Tackle. This did away with the winch vehicle by building the engine and mechanism into the plough frame. The outfit was winched between anchors on either side of the field. This photo dates from 1925

Probably the most significant event of all was the gradual appearance of diesel engines, particularly on European tractors, following early experiments by Benz in 1922. Several makes, notably Marshall and Garrett, were selling diesel tractors in Britain in 1930. Though most tractor engines were able to run on paraffin, this fuel greatly reduced their efficiency and also caused a complicated starting procedure which, if rushed and switched from petrol to paraffin before working temperature had been reached, meant a lengthy process whilst the fuel system was cleared of paraffin. The diesel did away with this problem and because of its efficiency was much cheaper to run. American tractors took longer to adopt diesels

(despite experiments by Allis-Chalmers in 1930) on account of the low cost of their petrol. Indeed, some American tractors did not even have paraffin carburettors even in the forties. However, their larger engined machines, notably crawlers, gradually followed Caterpillar's lead in 1931 with the 65 in offering diesels and International were offering WD-40 diesel wheeled tractors in 1935 in both America and Britain. The universal adoption of hydraulic lifts and mounted implements after the Second World War can be directly traced to Harry Ferguson's pioneer work in the thirties and the appearance of his Ferguson system tractor, built by David Brown from 1936.

Almost as significant as the diesel

engine and hydraulic implement control were the appearance of pneumatic rubber tyres on tractors in the early thirties. These were initially conversions using truck or aircraft tyres, but from 1933 several tyre manufacturers were making specially ribbed tractor tyres and these were fitted as standard by an increasing number of manufacturers in America from that year.

65 The Model D John Deere was joined in 1928 by the smaller GP [10/20 general purpose] tractor. This was particularly suited to rowcrop work with its high clearance front axle arrangement. Though other tractors, notably Emerson-Brantingham, had offered mechanical implement lifts, this model was the first popular one to do so. John Deere tractors were not actively marketed in Britain, following the demise of the Overtime, until the 1930's. They then disappeared again until 1962

66 An Irish Fordson N of 1930, loading tripod corn in Essex. With the end of American Fordson tractor production, the F was redesigned and introduced as the N early in 1929 from Ford's Cork factory. Its prime differences as compared with the F were an extra 1/8 inch in the cylinder bore, increasing its RAC horsepower to 27.28hp and magneto ignition with an impulse attachment to give easier starting. There were numerous detail improvements, including larger bearings, a sprung pivot on the front axle and an extra 10 quart capacity in the cooling system, with water pump built into the solid connection between the engine and radiator. The distinctive bulge on the rear mudguard was even more pronounced when first introduced and was claimed to reduce the likelihood of the tractor rearing over backwards - an unlikely claim in view of its sheet metal construction

Not only did pneumatic tyres increase operating speeds and enable tractors to move on the road without first having to unbolt spuds or retract strakes, but they allowed water ballast to be carried in them to increase traction when required. Fourteen percent of all tractors made in America in 1935 had pneumatic tyres and in 1940 this figure had risen to 95%.

68 Benz demonstrated the world's first agricultural tractor with a true diesel engine in 1922. It was a two cylinder 3 wheel machine and was followed by a four wheel version in 1923. Benz and Mercedes merged in 1926 and in 1930 one of the Mercedes single cylinder diesel tractors was shown in Britain by J & H McLaren Ltd. McLarens converted several steam ploughing engines to diesel power and also made a few tractors for direct ploughing with 16/27.5 twin cylinder Benz engines as opposed to the 14/20hp Mercedes-origin engine in the machine shown here

67A & B [Left]   The Rushton was an interesting attempt by a major British manufacturer to break the American dominance of mass-produced tractors on the British market in 1929. The shape of the Rushton badge gives an immediate clue to the backer, none other than the makers of AEC commercial vehicles. George Rushton was general manager of the Associated Equipment Co and convinced that his tractor could succeed. He used AEC's recently vacated factory [they had moved to Southall] at Walthamstow to produce the 14 drawbar horsepower, three forward speed tractor. A crawler version was also offered with optional six speed transmission and his export manager was Walter Hill, late of Muir-Hill. Unfortunately, it did not sell as anticipated and Rushton and AEC parted company, the tractor being offered for a time from Feltham, then St Ives, Huntingdonshire and finally by Tractors [London] Ltd of Tottenham, later to become known for their Trusty tractor. The Rushton was closely based on the Fordson and many of its parts were interchangeable. It first appeared in 1928 as the General, which was simply an 'improved' Fordson

69 The Garrett diesel tractor was a most enterprising machine for 1929 but sadly only seventeen were made before its makers got into financial difficulties in the Depression. Garretts of Leiston were members of the Agricultural and General Engineers group which included other famous old steam names like Aveling and Porter and Charles Burrell. Another member was Blackstone and Co Ltd, who had built crawlers until five years previously, and a choice of their 36/40hp or Aveling and Porter's Invicta 42hp diesels were offered.

Though heavy and expensive. the tractor in wheeled and crawler forms was undoubtedly good, as confirmed by one beating the continuous ploughing record in 1930 with a run of 977 hours, followed by a further 600 hours after it had been accidentally stalled

70 In 1930 Massey-Harris produced their first tractor designed by themselves as opposed to being a bought-in design like the Buda engined Parrett and the Wallis. The new Hercules engined Massey-Harris general purpose tractor was unusual in having all-wheel drive, though similar machines had been offered previously by smaller companies. It was built in a variety of widths, from 48ins to 76ins and its steering brakes could turn it within a six foot circle. Ground clearance of 30ins was achieved by the axles driving to the top edge of reduction gears on the wheels. The front axle was fixed and the rear axle free to pivot to compensate for uneven ground. It had a four cylinder 25hp engine and three forward gears and was built through much of the thirties with revised styling from 1936

71 The Lanz Bulldog was familiar in Britain in the thirties and was imported from the late twenties by the Locomobile Engineering Co, London, SW1. Its single cylinder had a colossal bore and stroke of 8-7/8x10¼ inches which gave it an RAC rating of 31.5hp. 30bhp was developed and drawbar pull was 2000 lbs, enabling it to pull 15 tons up a 1 in 34 hill in bottom gear. The engine ran on heavy oil and it relied on blow-lamp starting, after which the combustion process created its own ignition. Three forward gears were provided, giving up to 9 mph when on optionally available solid rubber tyres. The example shown [Model 22/38] dates from 1934. Lanz finally went over to full diesels in 1953

72 The four wheel drive and four wheel steer Latil timber and road haulage tractor from France was assembled in Britain for a time in the thirties by Shelvoke and Drewry [SD municipal vehicles]. From 1930 several attempts were made to interest farmers in its off-road abilities and retractable strakes were fitted to make ploughing possible. It had a six speed gearbox and the JTL version shown towing a Clayton combine in this 1930 photograph was rated at 17.9hp whilst the KTLA was of 20hp. At around £650 in 1930 it was not often bought for farming purposes, but has the distinction of being the first pneumatic tyred tractor available [1927]

73 The Farmall tractor from International Harvester first appeared in 1922 and entered production in 1924 and was intended to be able to do every conceivable farm job. It was given adjustable track and a high ground clearance [originally by hub reduction gearing] to enable it to work amongst row crops, and a centre steering arrangement so that it could have close-set front wheels for tricycle layout. The Farmall took some years to find favour with the farming community but after the first three years, during which time only 1114 were built, its production was moved to the Moline Plow Co's old works in Rock Island where it eventually built up to a grand production total of 420,460 by the end of 1938.

Shown is an F30, a model which joined the original 22.5hp Farmall in 1931 and was mechanically similar to the International W30. It was photographed with an Ann Arbor baler in Hampshire in 1932

74 The British designed but French built Austin tractor was relaunched in Britain in 1931 with a new enlarged engine [an extra 3/8ins in the cylinder bore] which now gave 20hp at the drawbar and 35 at the brake. Its three forward speeds gave up to 3.6 mph [previously over 6 mph] and it could handle a three to four furrow plough. It had grown in weight from the 28 cwt of the earliest Austin tractor to 36 cwt

75 [*Top*] The 20hp petrol/paraffin Caterpillar 20 first appeared in Britain in about 1930, following its American introduction in 1928, and here one is photographed in 1932, towing a pioneer British combine harvester, the Clayton and Shuttleworth. Clayton had been bought by Marshall in the mid-twenties and until the post-war Massey-Ferguson was the only significant combine made in Britain. This one worked on W R Warburton's farm in Oxfordshire and is remembered as an excellent machine. The story goes that Clayton were finally driven out of business when a consignment of uninsured combines for Argentina caught fire at the docks in Buenos Aires

76 Several small engineering firms cum blacksmiths built cheap tractors in the twenties and thirties, utilising redundant car components. The Model T Ford was frequently used as was the Morris Cowley shown here. This example was called the Beat-em-All and was produced in 1931 by Burnett and Wain of Rowsley, Derbyshire. It had a mounted cutter bar and a modified car axle which both drove the rear wheels by chain and also a belt pulley. The front wheels were simply standard car artillery type with the tyres removed!

77 [*Top*] One of the final attempts to interest farmers in steam traction was the Foden Agri-Tractor, which in 1931 was described as the most powerful and economical tractor in the world. It was widely exhibited overseas but only 3 were sold. It had two high pressure cylinders of 5x7 inch bore and stroke and two forward gears, giving up to 7½ mph. It could haul 12 tons or plough 12 acres per day. Unfortunately, Foden's days of

steam were numbered and their first diesel lorry sold in July 1931 soon put an end to their tractor attempts

78 Though of little significance to the British scene, it is interesting to compare the remarkably similar approach to tractor design being followed on the Continent by Lanz and OM in the thirties. Though outwardly similar to the

Marshall, with horizontal single cylinder engine, the Lanz and OM were hot bulb machines, whereas the Marshall was a full diesel. In 1968 OM or Officine Meccaniche became part of Fiat and produces trucks and engines, many of the latter being used in Fiat tractors. Other significant 1920's Italian tractors were the Landini [now owned by Massey-Ferguson] and Cassani [which was the forerunner of SAME]

79 The transverse engined Case models of the twenties were replaced by the in-line engined, unit-construction, three speed and reverse Models C and L in 1929, following J I Case Threshing Machine Co's acquisition of the Emerson-Brantingham Co in 1928. Shown is a 17/27hp Model C of about 1934, whilst the L was rated at 25/40hp.

Case tractors built up a good reputation in Britain following the appearance of Models C and L at the World Tractor Trials near Wantage in 1930. Their earlier appearance at the post-Great War tractor trials was not so fortunate because of intense competition and price cutting

80 Allis-Chalmers made tractors from 1915 but apart from a few imported into Britain during the Great War, little was heard of the company in British farming circles until the 1930's. One of the first models then was the excellent Model U shown here in 1934 towing an eleven inch single furrow Ransomes plough with 19 inch subsoiler. This model owed its origins to the United tractor [hence U] that was a co-operative manufacturing/marketing venture by a number of American agricultural firms in 1929. Allis-Chalmers was a member of the consortium and they produced the tractor, though engines came from Continental. Not a great deal came of the venture except that it gave birth to the long-lived Model U with Allis-Chalmers' own engine

81 The little Caterpillar Ten appeared in Britain in 1930 at the World Tractor Trials near Wantage, where it successfully handled a three furrow plough. Here is the seldom seen High Clearance row-crop version, introduced in 1931, with narrow tracks and 22 inch ground clearance, photographed at King's Lynn in 1934. Rated at 10hp it cost £320 and was a mere 8ft 4ins long. Three forward gears were provided and final drive was by spur gear.

At this time Caterpillar sales were handled in Britain by a company associated with the manufacturers of Thornycroft lorries, just as the Cletrac had been imported by the makers of Burford lorries

82 A cracked glass negative does little to detract from this fascinating example of the new replacing the old. The new in this case is a Massey-Harris 25/40, first introduced in 1933, which had been bought by Mr Yeomans, a Hertfordshire farmer, to replace the portable steam engine in the foreground. Note the shafts which allowed the steam engine to be towed by horses. Following the acquisition of the Wallis tractor design in 1927, Massey's first own-design tractor was their 4x4 in 1930, followed by this more conventional 25/40 which was closely related to the Wallis

83 In 1929 the Oliver Chilled Plow Works of South Bend, Indiana, which had not previously produced tractors, changed its name to the Oliver Farm Equipment Co after merging with a number of other implement makers. Amongst these was the Hart-Parr Co of Charles City, Iowa, which had made tractors since 1902 and was credited with some of the first farm tractors in America after the pioneering Huber and Kinnaird Haines [Flour City] designs of 1897/8. The Hart-Parr range of horizontal engined tractors was discontinued in favour of a new Oliver Hart-Parr vertical engined range, amongst the earliest of which were special Row Crop tricycle tractors from 1930 and the conventional 18/28 shown here, photographed in England in 1934, which developed into the Oliver 80

84   With the end of Blackstone and Clayton crawler tractor production in the early twenties, the market was dominated by Cletrac and Caterpillar until the introduction of the Fowler in the early thirties. This is a 1933 Diesel 25 which bore a close resemblance to [some would say, was a copy of] the Caterpillar 28, one of the American company's least successful models on account of problems with dust seals. The Fowler was soon revised as the 3/30 with a similar 30hp 3 cylinder Fowler-Sanders diesel to the 25.

This example belonged to R H Crawford of Frithville, near Boston, Lincs, who bought it for his farm and then took out a Fowler agency. He is still selling its descendant, the Aveling-Marshall today

85   Following the end of American Fordson tractor production, they were made at Cork from 1929 to 1932, when they were moved to the new Dagenham plant near London. This is a 1934 example demonstrating an early Ford experiment with mechanically driven and raised direct-mounted implements - in this case the Tillivator. Irish Fordson production had been badly hit by the slump from 50 a day in 1930 when several thousand Irish Fords had been sent to the United States to 3501 in 1931 and 3060 in 1932. [Initial Dagenham production was 2778 in 1933 and 3582 in 1934]

86 The Allis-Chalmers WC general purpose tractor was launched in 1934 and here one tows a trailer and Bamfords hay loader in 1935. The WC was one of the first new models to be offered with pneumatic tyres from the outset following experiments with specially adapted Firestone aircraft tyres from 1932. To publicise them, a Model U averaged 17½ mph for five hours, whilst another suitably geared was driven by Barney Oldfield at 64.28 mph in 1933.

The WC model was classed as a 2/3 furrow machine and had a four cylinder 12/20hp engine and four forward gears

87 The International/McCormick-Deering W30 appeared in 1932 and continued until 1940, by which time just over 32,000 had been made and 1300 sold in Britain.

It had a four cylinder petrol/paraffin engine, developing 19.7hp at the drawbar and 31.3hp on the belt and was intended for farms of over 200 acres. It had four forward speeds, giving up to 4 mph, though a special ratio for pneumatic tyred W30s gave 10 mph

88 A single cylinder two stroke diesel Marshall powers a Ransomes threshing machine in about 1934, whilst an International 22/36 feeds it with sheafed corn. The Marshall appears to be an early 18/30 model [with Bosch in place of Marshall fuel pump] with slightly more rounded fuel tank than its predecessor, the 15/30, which had first appeared in public at the World Tractor Trials near Wantage in 1930. It was hand started [no easy matter with early bore and stroke measurements of 8ins x 10½ins] with the aid of a glow paper or cigarette end. It was an unusual machine and with gradual modification and refinement it was produced until 1957

89 An unfamiliar tractor to British eyes, as only 20 were imported [1934-38] was the McCormick-Deering Fairway 12 for golf courses and playing fields. It shared the same engine as the W-12 and Farmall F-12 but had the same gear ratio as the orchard model International 0-12 which gave up to 7½ mph in place of about 4 mph on the standard tractors.

More common on British golf courses were the tractors made by Allan Taylor of Wandsworth and Moxon and Pattisson and usually based on Ford T, A and B components

90 Ransomes and Rapier Ltd of Ipswich made a variety of crawler tractors in the thirties with the name Rapier to avoid confusion with their well-known agricultural neighbours Ransomes, Sims and Jefferies Ltd. Their first machine was a two ton tractor in 1934 with two cylinder Ailsa Craig 15hp engine. Then at the Royal Agricultural Show in 1934 they unveiled their RT50 eight ton machine powered by a Dorman-Ricardo four cylinder 50/65hp diesel. It had Roadless rubber joined tracks and six forward gears. The example shown here in 1936 was able to draw a six furrow plough and cover ten acres per day in Suffolk. Very few were made and the company soon concentrated on cranes and other constructional machinery

91 Caterpillar made one of the first diesel crawlers in the world in 1931, the 65, and in 1933 several other smaller models in their range could also be diesel powered. The Forty shown had a three cylinder 40hp diesel and was built in about 1935. The photograph was taken in the Lincolnshire Fens in 1940 and shows a two furrow plough set at one foot depth with a nine inch subsoiler. Front and rear lamps for night ploughing are fitted.
  The Caterpillar Tractor Co had been formed in Illinois in 1925 as a result of the merger of the C L Best Tractor Co and the Holt Manufacturing Co [holders of the Caterpillar trademark] both of whom had made competitive crawlers

92 Based on the International/McCormick-Deering W12, the Farmall F12 rowcrop and multi-purpose tractor joined the larger Farmall F20 [which had replaced the original Farmall Regular in 1931] and F30 in 1932 and grew into the F14 in 1938. 123,500 F12 and F14 were built in all and it was a popular small machine in Britain. The F12 had three forward gears and a four cylinder engine developing 10/15hp. It was rated as a one furrow plough tractor though two furrows were feasible in most ground conditions and became standard with the more powerful F14. All Farmalls were grey with red wheels until 1st November 1936, when they became red all over, a colour continued on the new A, B, H and M models in 1939. The example shown is fitted with optional pneumatic tyres, though steel wheels were more commonly seen in Britain

93A, B & C The Gyrotiller in action in the mid-thirties. These are examples of the largest model which had six cylinder engines [some, MAN and Fowler-Sanders diesels] of 150 to 180hp. The smaller 3 cyl 30hp, 4 cyl 40 and 6 cyl 80 did not have front steering wheels. Several contractors ran them and they moved around the country in much the same way as the old steam ploughing sets. Unfortunately, they went out of fashion in the late thirties as a result of often being set to cultivate too deep. This upset the subsoil and caused drainage problems as well as making the soil too spongy to be worked by horses or tractors in wet weather

94 In 1935 Cletrac introduced their Model E, a compact crawler for a variety of cultivation purposes including up to four furrow ploughing. It was available in five widths to cater for various row-crop requirements. Shown is the smallest 31 inch or 38 inch version whilst up to 76 inches was offered.

The Cleveland Tractor Co had been founded in 1916 to promote machines developed from 1911 by the two White brothers, of steam and petrol car and truck making fame. The Cletrac, along with the small Caterpillars, were the most successful tracklayers in Britain in the twenties and thirties, the Cletrac being sold for many years as the Burford-Cletrac in honour of H G Burford, the importer

95 In 1936 the 12/20 Marshall became the Model M, which continued until 1945. It differed from the earlier model primarily in its more streamlined appearance with its radiator now moved sideways like the Lanz. Here a 1938 Model M powers a Foster threshing machine which is equipped with a stack feeder for loading sheafs. The Marshall was particularly suited to such stationary duties as its engine could run indefinitely under full load consuming less than a gallon of diesel fuel per hour

96 The Fordson N or Standard model remained in production from 1929 to 1945 with detail modifications and was the backbone to much of Britain's mechanised farming. This typical late summer scene shows a standard Fordson on pneumatic tyres [note the special cast iron Goodyear wheels] drawing an Albion No 8 reaper/binder. From late 1937 most Fordsons were orange in place of their former blue but were green from 1940 onwards

97 The well-known implement makers Ransomes, Sims and Jefferies Ltd of Ipswich produced their first light crawler tractor in 1936 and this is an early example with Sturmey-Archer/Raleigh 6bhp air cooled four stroke single cylinder engine. It had an automatic clutch and single forward and reverse gears and was able to exert a 600 lbs drawbar pull. It weighed 9½ cwt and cost only £135. It was popular in market gardens and smallholdings and remained in production for well over twenty years, acquiring such improvements as three forward and reverse gears and hydraulic lift

98 Harry Ferguson was a gifted Ulster inventor who regarded the traditional use of the tractor as a simple substitute for the horse with its primitive implements as totally unsatisfactory. During the First World War he designed a mounted plough whose geometry forced both the front and back wheels of the towing vehicle onto the ground in a scientifically balanced manner which overcame the traditional tendency of the plough to lift the front wheels in heavy going. This was exhibited to Henry Ford, who was anxious to exploit Ferguson's talents. However, Ferguson did not want to be an employee and he continued perfecting his idea, eventually patenting a system whereby quickly detachable mounted implements would work at a pre-ordained depth, constantly monitored by a hydraulic pump and load sensing device. Both Rushton and Ransomes and Rapier proposed to incorporate the idea on their tractors, but neither was in a strong enough position to promote it as Ferguson wanted. In the end, Ferguson built his own prototype lightweight tractor in 1933 with a Hercules four cylinder engine to prove his whole integrated tractor and implement system. It was extremely successful and in 1936 the first production example, shown here, was made by David Brown

99 David Brown took on the production of the new Ferguson in 1936 because they were anxious to diversify and already knew a lot about the prototype, having supplied it with gears. In place of the original Hercules engine, the 18/20hp Coventry Climax unit was fitted to the first 550 and thereafter the remaining 700 had an engine developed by David Brown. As shown in this 1937 demonstration, the Ferguson draft control system worked in all conditions and maintained the implement at a uniform depth automatically, even when the tractor's rear wheels were in a hollow. Unfortunately, the tractor was slow to sell, costing roughly twice as much as a Fordson when the special implements it had to use were taken into account. It was also too small for many farmers so David Brown, against Ferguson's wishes, decided to produce a more powerful version. Meanwhile Ferguson demonstrated a 'Ferguson-Brown' tractor to Henry Ford in America in an effort to persuade him to mass produce it and thereby reduce its cost

100 This Allis-Chalmers WF of around 1937 was a smaller tractor than the U and had a four cylinder engine with a common bore and stroke of four inches as compared with 4-3/8x 5ins of the contemporary U. It had four forward speeds, giving up to 9 mph. This example was photographed in England during August 1938 and is towing a Ransome's rigid tine cultivator. Allis-Chalmers took the British market seriously and had established a large warehouse at Southampton to supply spares and equipment shipped from their American factories which had a total ground area of 493 acres

101 A 1936 Oliver Hart-Parr 70 Row-Crop hoeing in a field of Brussels sprouts. This model was introduced in 1935 and though available in conventional form was most common in Britain as a row-crop tractor. It had a six cylinder overhead valve engine of 23/28hp with electric self starter. The 70 model number related to the octane of the petrol it would run on, though a paraffin version [70KD] was available. The 70 was revised in 1939 and given a six forward speed gearbox

102 In the late thirties a large selection of two wheel market garden and small holding tractors appeared. One of the best known was the British Anzani Iron Horse. It was made from 1938 for some twenty years and featured a JAP six horsepower four stroke single cylinder engine and a three forward and reverse speed gearbox. Steering was effected by clutch controls for each wheel mounted on both handlebars. It could travel at up to 4½ mph and consumed under two gallons of petrol per day

103 The Allis-Chalmers Model M was the crawler version of their U wheeled tractor. The M is believed to have stood for Monarch, the Monarch Tractor Co, makers of a range of American crawlers, having been taken over in 1928. An A-C Monarch diesel crawler was experimented with as early as 1930. Another Allis-Chalmers acquisition [in 1931] was that of Advance-Rumely, famed for their OilPull tractors and at that time one of the few firms offering a large conventional six cylinder model, the Rumely '6'.

This photograph shows a Model M in the early years of the war, demonstrating a Darby Digger to R S Hudson, the Minister of Agriculture. Though equipped with the same engine as the U, the M's was rated at 28/35hp. It had four forward and one reverse gear and was capable of nearly 6 mph

THE SECOND WORLD WAR AND AFTER

Just as in 1914/18, the Second World War provided an enormous impetus for tractor growth. Britain had to be increasingly self-sufficient in her food supply and once more relied on the import of thousands of American tractors to help achieve this.
However, unlike the First World War, she now had a few active home producers, notably Ford and David Brown.

104   A 1940 International TD6 TracTracTor at work in Northamptonshire in the early years of the Second World War. It had a four cylinder diesel engine and five forward speed gearbox. Also available was the similar T6 30hp paraffin engined crawler. From 1953 the TD6 was made in Britain as the 40hp [50hp from 1955] BTD6 [though with an indirect injection diesel as opposed to the petrol-start split-head type in the TD6] and the T6 was also produced at Doncaster in petrol and paraffin versions

After the war, increasingly intensive agricultural methods brought mechanisation to the smallest farms and market gardens and there were several new light tractors produced in Britain. By far the most important of these was the Ferguson, made in Coventry from 1946. Another important newcomer was Morris for the first time with their Nuffield range in 1948. Several popular American makes disappeared from the British scene following 1945, but those that had done best here, like International and Allis-Chalmers, soon began to make tractors in Britain. Ford at Dagenham replaced their ageing N model in 1945 with the Major, having never made the Ford-Ferguson in Britain as Harry Ferguson had hoped.

In the fifties, diesel engines finally won the day and more or less all post-war tractors were designed with hydraulic implement lifts.

Enclosed tractor cabs gradually appeared following one of the first on the market from Minneapolis Moline in 1938.

Tractors grew in power but were technically little different from those produced by the larger companies in the thirties, though the torque converter transmission on Allis-Chalmers' 1947 HD19 crawler was an interesting new development, even if better suited to earthmoving than agricultural tractors. In fact, tractor transmission changed little until the mid-fifties, apart from acquiring two, three, then four crash ratios as compared with the earliest single speed designs. After that, synchromesh and epicyclic splitters increased the number of ratios available and simplified gear shifting on the move.

In this final section we have strayed little beyond 1955 and have only shown some of the more unusual or most important post-war models to give an idea of the enormous strides that tractor design had taken in just fifty short years.

105 A pair of Cletrac BG or BD models ploughing in Surrey in 1940. Rated at approximately 35hp the G stood for gasoline and the D for diesel, the engines being supplied by Continental and Hercules respectively. Cletrac's first diesel machine had appeared in 1933 as the Diesel 80 and diesel tractors down to 35hp were offered in the following year. The Cleveland Tractor Co remained independent until bought by the Oliver Corp in 1944. Ironically this firm was eventually acquired by White in the early sixties, whose founders had originally designed the Cleveland Motor Plow

106 The Oliver 90 was the biggest of Oliver's pre-war range and took over from the 28/44 in 1937. It was classed as a three to five plough machine and its four cylinder engine developed 29/45hp. It started with three forward gears but acquired four in 1939. This photograph was taken in 1942 and shows manure being loaded on a 19ft trailer

107 Four types of motive power in use in Northumberland in 1940. In the foreground are Caterpillar R2 and Ferguson A [made by Ferguson-Brown Tractors Ltd - David Brown Tractors and Harry Ferguson Ltd were formally merged in June 1937]. In the background is a Case CC rowcrop machine

108 Though production of the International 10/20 officially ended in 1940 after a run of seventeen years, it continued to be available in Britain until 1942. Here is one of the last, driving a strawpress from its belt pulley. The 10/20 was generally regarded as the first quality engineered and well-made modern tractor on the British market and was about 50% more expensive than the contemporary Fordson

109 This Farmall A seen in Wiltshire in 1940 was the smallest in the new Farmall range introduced in 1939. It was available with an extra 6 inches ground clearance as the AV and in tricycle form as the B. All had the same 17/19hp four cylinder petrol engine and Culti-Vision, in which the operator had a direct view of the ground in front of him for delicate row-crop work. This was achieved by off-setting the engine in the A and AV and the driving position on the much wider B. The example shown here was photographed in Wiltshire in 1941

110 Massey-Harris introduced their 81, 101 Junior, 101 Senior, 201, 202 and 203 models in 1939. They had six cylinder Chrysler or Continental engines, except the four cylinder 81 and 101 Junior, and so-called Twin-Power in which different governor settings could be selected to gain extra revs and power.

This 201 three/four furrow model is shown working near Bridgwater in 1943 with a self-lift drag harrow.

Massey-Harris finally merged with Ferguson in 1953 and subsequently bought the Perkins diesel engine company in 1959, the Italian Landini tractor firm in 1960 and the earthmoving machinery side of Hanomag [a few of whose agricultural crawlers were sold in Britain in the fifties] in 1974. They also have a financial interest in the Ebro and Eicher tractor firms

111 The John Deere range was restyled in 1938 along the lines shown here on this 1942 BN ridging potatoes. The Model B had first appeared in 1935 as a one furrow plough tractor [the A, introduced in 1934, was its bigger two furrow sister]. In 1934 John Deere had been pioneers of hydraulic implement lifts [though these, of course, did not incorporate 3 point linkage as draft control]. From 1938 the B was a high rowcrop machine with twin trike front wheels. Other versions were the BN [in which N meant narrow, rowcrop single front wheel], BR [low, standard build, fixed axle], BW [wide, adjustable front axle four wheeler], BO [as BR but shielded for orchards] and BV [vineyard]. These suffix letters also applied to the A range. This BN was a light 'two plough' capacity 16/20hp machine with four forward speeds giving up to 5¼ mph.

John Deere remained faithful to their horizontal engine layout right up to 1962 and even made it in diesel form from 1949. There was one exception, however - the small L model and its derivatives of 1939 had vertical twins

112 The Minneapolis-Moline Power Implement Co was formed in 1929 with the merger of the Minneapolis Threshing Machine Co [Minneapolis tractors], Minneapolis Steel and Machinery Co [Twin City tractors] and Moline Plow Co [who had made the Moline tractor until 1924]. Little was heard of Minneapolis-Moline in Britain until the arrival of World War II when their tractors became familiar on British farms and shown here is a Model ZTU in Somerset. The letter Z indicated a 21/28hp model, first introduced in the United States in 1937, TU indicated V twin-wheel tricycle, TN single tricycle front wheel, TS wide fixed track front axle and TE wide extendable track front axle

113 J I Case increased their production capacity by buying the Rock Island Plow Co in 1937, the former makers of the Heider and Rock Island tractors. Then in 1939 they introduced a new streamlined D and R, followed by S, LA and V ranges, with the identifying colour scheme of flambeau red. The three plough capacity D came with a number of options to suit special purposes, such as row crop [DC] and orchard [DO] and had a mechanical implement lift. Rated at 26/32hp with Case's own engine, it was joined by the smaller S and Continental engined V in the early years of the war and by a new 4/5 plough model, the LA, in 1941. The full range of D models was D, DC3 [tricycle], DC4 [wide axle], DEX [hybrid], DO,DV [vineyard] and DR [rice].

The D shown here is a wartime example working in 1951 with a New Holland 80 baler.

Case disappeared from the British scene for a time after the Second World War but are now firmly entrenched once more, having bought the David Brown tractor firm in 1972

114 The Farmall Model H was one of the new range that replaced the F series in 1939 and a 1941 example is shown. The H had a four cylinder petrol/paraffin engine of 25hp and five forward gears giving up to 16 mph on rubbers. Its belt and drawbar horsepower ratings were within 6% of each other thanks to the liberal use of low friction ball and roller bearings. The largest of the range was the M of 37hp and its diesel derivative, the MD, of 31/36hp. The diesel model was not imported into Britain

115 An Oliver 80 Standard, photographed in 1940 dragging out gorse bushes in Devon prior to ploughing. The 80 was a four cylinder machine developed from the old 18/28 and now rated at approximately 23/33hp. It had four forward gears and a maximum drawbar pull in bottom gear of 5079 lbs at 2.41 mph.

In 1944 the Oliver Farm Equipment Co merged with the Cleveland Tractor Co to form the Oliver Corporation. The Cletrac name was discontinued and in 1960 the company was acquired by the White Motor Corporation, who also bought Minneapolis-Moline

116 A Caterpillar D4 made during the Second World War at work with a disc harrow in Hampshire. Like the D2 the D4 had five forward gears and a 10hp two cylinder petrol starter motor. Its diesel engine, however, developed 36/41hp, which gave it a maximum drawbar pull of almost 8000 lbs against 6000 lbs for the D2

117 A Minneapolis-Moline two plough capacity Model ZTS in Oxfordshire in 1940 with an M-M combine harvester. M-M engines incorporated a number of unfamiliar features, like horizontal valves worked by long rocker arms from a low-mounted camshaft. Various compression ratios were available and indeed on the 1937 Model Z they could be altered in the field to suit varying fuel qualities. Another advanced M-M feature was the option of operators' cabs on certain models from 1938

118 David Brown had been pressing on with their more powerful version of the Ferguson VAK 1 and with the departure of Ferguson to America this became the first David Brown tractor in July 1939. A 1944 version of the original VAK model is shown here, working a mid-mounted hydraulically controlled Stanhay hoe. It had four forward speeds and two independent hand brakes.

The VAK incorporated a built-in power take off which David Brown had wanted on their Ferguson, but had instead made do with a bolt-on accessory. The VAK was built onto a steel trough frame in place of full unit construction and had 35 bhp 2½ litre petrol engine with overhead valves and wet liners.

Meanwhile Harry Ferguson had persuaded Henry Ford to produce his tractor and in 1939 the Ford with Ferguson system appeared, looking very much like the familiar British post-war Standard-built Ferguson. It was designated 9N when petrol engined, 9NAN paraffin and 2N utility

119 The Fowler Diesel 25, which became the 3/30, was replaced in 1945/6 by the broadly similar FD3, still with Fowler-Sanders 35hp 3 cylinder diesel. A four cylinder FD2 version was also made concurrently until both were discontinued in 1947 following the acquisition of the company by Thos W Ward, who already controlled Marshalls of Gainsborough. During the war Fowlers had been owned by the Ministry of Supply, followed by Mr Howard of Rotovator fame.

The example shown is towing a large 49 tine Australian Suntyne drill, which had been imported to Britain in 1935 and been drilling 1000 acres per year ever since

120 A big 48hp four cylinder International W9 at work in North Shropshire in 1944, where it was able to plough 16 acres per day using 1½ gallons of fuel per hour. The W9 replaced the W40 [introduced in 1935] in 1940 and continued until 1953. It was also available with a diesel engine as the WD9, though none of the latter were sold in Britain. It was regarded as an excellent tractor for belt work though it was too large, and lacking in traction for most normal farm work in Britain, but was widely used for breaking rough land during the war to increase food production and for replacing traction engines in threshing

121 A crawler version of the David Brown tractor was produced during the war using a four cylinder Dorman engine. It was based on the Caterpillar D4 and around two hundred were made for the Ministry of Supply. After the war it was completely redesigned as the 30 and 40 with David Brown's own four and six cylinder engines. This photograph was taken in 1945

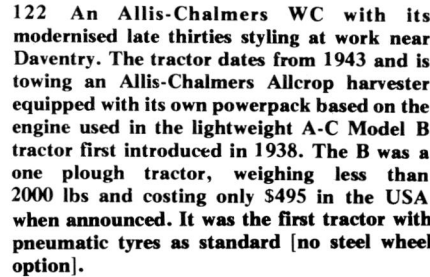

122 An Allis-Chalmers WC with its modernised late thirties styling at work near Daventry. The tractor dates from 1943 and is towing an Allis-Chalmers Allcrop harvester equipped with its own powerpack based on the engine used in the lightweight A-C Model B tractor first introduced in 1938. The B was a one plough tractor, weighing less than 2000 lbs and costing only $495 in the USA when announced. It was the first tractor with pneumatic tyres as standard [no steel wheel option].

Note the land girl on the harvester, one of thousands who helped to alleviate the wartime manpower shortage

123 The Minneapolis-Moline GTA was one of the largest wheeled tractors in Britain during the Second World War. It was rated at 36/49hp and could handle up to five furrow ploughing. Normally on rubber tyres all round, this example in Dorset has been converted to spade lug wheels because of the shortage of rubber in the war. Pneumatics were limited to users having to travel on the road, such as threshing contractors. M-M bought the makers of the Avery tractor, occasionally seem in Britain during the war [B F Avery of Louisville, not Avery Co of Peoria, who went out of business in 1941] in 1950 and in 1961 they were, in turn, acquired by the White Motor Corporation, along with Oliver

124 A Standard Fordson converted to Roadless DG half tracks by Bomford and Evershed of Salford Priors, near Evesham, during the Second World War. The front axle is 1944 pattern but the fuel mixer is earlier, suggesting that the machine has seen considerable service and been gradually modified. Some tractors of the time were given half tracks to reduce ground pressure and increase traction, and many of these went to the Forces. From late 1937 most Fordsons were orange instead of their former blue but from 1940 they were usually painted green

125 This special purpose one-off tractor was made by G Manton of Stroxton, Grantham, in 1945. It was based on a Crossley 4x4 chassis powered by an engine from an Allis-Chalmers WF tractor and shows typical agricultural ingenuity at a time of machinery and tractor shortages

126 The International W6 and its diesel sister, the WD6, were made from 1940 to 1953. Rated at 36 belt hp they had five forward gears but, in common with other USA tractors, top could only be used if the tractor was fitted with pneumatic tyres. This example is shown towing a self-powered International baler during the Second World War, in the days when the wire still had to be tied by hand

127 A Caterpillar D2 at work with a Ransomes earth scoop in 1944 making a silage pit. In the background is a Fowler earth scoop of the type used in the widening of the Suez Canal.

The D2 was introduced specifically for agricultural use in 1938. It could handle a three/four furrow plough and was powered by a four cylinder diesel engine of 26 drawbar and 32 belt horsepower. Speeds of up to 5 mph were possible in top [fifth] gear. A horizontally opposed twin cylinder 10hp petrol engine was used as a starter motor and these donkey starters were standard on all Cat diesels

128   The Oliver 60 first appeared in 1939 and differed from the outwardly similar 70 in that it had four [later five] forward gears and a four cylinder engine. With the end of wartime Lend-Lease no more Olivers came to Britain, though this photograph of a Row Crop 60 with Leverton duster was taken in 1947. The name Hart-Parr had been discontinued on Oliver tractors in 1937. Some of the final small Olivers were, in fact, made for the company by David Brown from 1960 and later Fiat, though large tractors are still produced by Oliver, usually under the name White

129   Although tractors ran on cruder fuel than most other vehicles, it was vital to reduce the consumption of imported fuel during the Second World War. As a result various attempts were made to run vehicles on producer gas and in this 1945 experiment at the National Institute of Agricultural Engineering at Askham Bryan College of Agriculture a Standard Fordson has been equipped to produce its own gas in the anthracite burner mounted on the right of the machine

130 Following the acquisition of Fowler by Thos W Ward, who already owned Marshall, the three and four cylinder Fowlers were discontinued in 1947 and replaced by the VF model, which used Marshall's well-known single cylinder two stroke diesel. Here a Fowler Marshall British Diesel pulls a Crawford two furrow, one-way plough in December 1948. The VF was modified as the VFA, which continued to be produced until replaced by the Perkins engined Track-Marshall in 1957

131 The Allis-Chalmers HD10 was one of a range of crawlers introduced in 1940 equipped with General Motors two stroke vertical diesel engines. There was also an HD7 and an HD14, the numbers indicating the number of furrows that the tractor could turn. They had three, four and six cylinder engines of 57, 82 and 127 drawbar horsepower. This example arrived in Lincolnshire in 1946/47 and is seen here with a three furrow plough on marshy land

132 Another development in the forties was small mechanised tool frames designed to take the backbreaking manual labour out of tending vegetables. This is a 1947 Bean [no relation to the car and lorry maker of 1919-31 with the same name] with 10hp Ford engine and hand lever adjusted frame height. It was first made in 1946 in the market garden area near Brough, E Yorks, by Blackburn Aircraft and its production was taken up in the fifties by Thomas Green & Son Ltd of Leeds. Mr Bean is still a large scale market gardener and the main grower of cucumbers in Britain with substantial export trade

133 Vivian Loyd of bren gun carrier design fame introduced this tractor in 1945 based on Ford V8 engine, running on petrol, was too thirsty and production models had Turner, Meadows and Dorman engines. They had tracks made by Marshall and were known as Dragons. Production ended in the early fifties

134 Numerous new firms entered the British tractor industry in the years immediately following the Second World War. The Byron Row Crop tractor was made by a respected name in agricultural machinery and grain augers, Byron Farm Machinery of London. It had a brief existence from 1947 and featured the industrial version of the Ford 10 engine so popular with light tractor makers at the time

135 The Ferguson TE20. Ford in Detroit, who had not made tractors in America since the late twenties, had a somewhat stormy relationship with Harry Ferguson while they made tractors incorporating Ferguson's hydraulic system from 1939 to 1946. These were sold to Harry Ferguson Inc for resale to the agricultural trade. Ford would have preferred to do a complete manufacturing/marketing job themselves and as Ferguson was not willing to sell his company to them, and thereby see the name Ferguson disappear, and could not persuade Ford to make his tractors in Britain, a rift finally came in November 1946. At this stage Ford had built 306,072 9Ns with their own 23.9 belt horse-power engine and three speed transmission.

Meanwhile, Ferguson had found a manu-facturer in Britain willing to make his tractor and the first TE20 [Tractor England] left the Standard Motor Company's Banner Lane works in Coventry in 1946. It was almost identical in appearance to the 9N but had four forward gears and a slightly more powerful Continental engine. Ford introduced their new 8N which was so closely based on the old 9N that Ferguson took legal action against them and was awarded £3 million. In fact, Harry Ferguson had cribbed the Ford tractor in much the same way that they had cribbed his hydraulics

136 The Bristol Tractor Company [originally an offshoot of Roadless Traction Ltd and founded by Walter Hill, late of Muir-Hill and Rushton] was formed in 1932 to market light crawler tractors built for them by the well-known Bristol motorcycle manufacturer, Douglas. Initially, they had horizontally opposed 1200cc air cooled Douglas engines but following an interest taken in the firm in 1933 by a member of the Jowett car making family, Jowett 7hp two cylinder water cooled engines were offered, as well as Coventry Victor 10hp diesels. Three forward gears were provided and a drawbar pull of 2000 lbs was available from each engine. Later the company was acquired by H A Saunders, the Austin dealers, and after the war Austin 10 and A70 engines were fitted, followed by Perkins diesels. The firm eventually became part of Marshalls of Gainsborough in the early seventies and their staple model was then renamed the Track Marshall 1100. In 1976 Marshalls were bought by Leyland and their tractors renamed Aveling-Marshall.

The example shown here was photographed in 1947 and was steered by levers in place of the tiller used on early models. The square nosed design replaced the original bull-nose in 1937

137 David Brown were scarcely established at their new Meltham tractor works when war was declared in 1939. Much of their subsequent tractor production went to the RAF and Navy for heavy towing duties and with peace in sight this Threshing Model was adapted from the tow tractor by the addition of a forward-mounted belt pulley. The agricultural model developed from the original VAK 1 [Vehicle Agricultural Kerosene, model 1] became the Cropmaster in 1947 [VAK 1A 1945, VAK 1C 1947] and the model shown here in 1945 soon developed into the industrial Taskmaster

138 The English Fordson N or Standard model ended its long production run in 1945 to be replaced by the E27N Major. In fact the Major was mechanically very similar to the Standard model and had the same engine, the principal differences being larger wheels, new final drive arrangement and, available soon afterwards, three-point hydraulic lift. The example shown here in 1952 with retractable strakes is spreading lime on Plynlimon to encourage grass growth for the Black cattle which live on the mountains all the year round

139 An important newcomer to the tractor scene in 1948 was the Nuffield from Morris. William Morris, who became Lord Nuffield in 1938, had formed Nuffield Mechanisations in 1936 to produce military vehicles. After the war the company needed new work and the swords to plough shares Nuffield tractor was developed. Rated at 30hp and with five forward speeds giving up to 16 mph, it had a hydraulic lift and power take-off from new. The 1948 example shown here is towing a Ford Ransomes plough

140 Two of the most familiar new light tractors after the war were the BMB President and the Ota shown here. Neither achieved much commercial success in the face of the much more sophisticated Ferguson. The President had the backing of the giant Brockhouse engineering group and in final Morris 918cc engined form disappeared in 1956. The Ota from Oak Tree Appliances of Coventry was developed in the late forties with a Ford 10 industrial engine. Its three forward speeds gave up to 15 mph and a hydraulic lift was offered from 1951. In 1952 a four wheel Monarch version was introduced with six forward speeds and this was adopted by Singer Motors as a serious attempt to rival Ferguson. It is doubtful whether it would have retained a Ford engine for long in view of its new parentage. However, it was outclassed by the Ferguson and Allis-Chalmers B and, following Singer's takeover by Rootes in 1956, it was quietly discontinued

141 The Farmall M petrol or petrol/paraffin and MD diesel tractors first appeared in the USA in 1939 and were extremely popular in Britain during the Second World War. From 1949 the 36/39hp M was produced in England at Doncaster as the BM and was joined by the 31/36hp BMD in 1952. From 1953 the BMD was offered as the Super BMD [43/48hp] and the BM became the Super BM 36/40hp vaporising oil tractor in 1954.

International expanded their British production capacity still further in the fifties with the acquisition of the Jowett factory at Idle, Bradford.

This Super BMD is shown baling rye grass and clover in a 1954 demonstration

142 After their unsuccessful attempt to break into the tractor market after the 1914/18 War the Garner lorry firm made a second and rather more successful attempt in 1947. This time they made the tractor themselves using an air cooled, single cylinder 6hp JAP engine. It started as a two wheel horticultural machine but in 1949 evolved into a rear engined four wheeler. Production was up to 15 per week and the machine was available with an air cooled twin cylinder 10hp engine in its final form in 1955. The 1949 example shown here has rear and mid-mounted toolbars

143 Unlike most of the new entries into the post-war tractor market who made lightweight machines, the respected gearbox makers, Turner Manufacturing Co of Wolverhampton took a leaf out of their gear competitor David Brown's book and produced a full-size machine. Their Yeoman of England tractor was announced in 1949 and was produced for approximately ten years. It was advertised as 'the wheeled tractor with crawler tractor performance' and featured Turner's own make of 68° V4 diesel engine, developing 32/40hp [the heads of one bank can be seen protruding from the side of the bonnet in this 1952 photograph]. The engine was designed by Freeman Sanders, who was also responsible for the Fowler diesel and Ferguson TEF20 engines. Its four forward gears gave up to 17 mph and its drawbar pull was 5500 lbs. It proved to be a fair tractor but suffered from transmission breakages and was too expensive to be justified for many agricultural purposes, except when used intensively by contractors

144 There was a serious shortage of heavy crawler tractors after the 1939/45 war and one enterprising contractor in Lincolnshire, Robert Crawford, converted this Sherman tank in 1948 to tow a 1914 Fowler balance plough. It could handle a three foot single furrow or five/six furrow conventional plough and could travel at 30 mph between sites. He also used a converted Valentine tank with single 130hp GMC engine [the Sherman had two]

145   In 1945 the Marshall M was replaced by the Series I which had a differential lock for maximum traction in difficult conditions. Shown here is the Series II, made from 1947 to '49, and now equipped with steering brakes [note the operating levers beside the wings]. The final versions were the III from 1949 to 1952 and the IIIA from 1952 to '57, when Marshall finally discontinued single cylinder tractors. Tracked versions were also marketed under the Fowler name. The IIIA had an engine swept volume of 4894cc [6½ x 9ins bore and stroke] and produced 40bhp at its governed maximum of 750 rpm. [Its audible detonation led to the Marshall's nickname of the Pom-Pom tractor.] A two ratio gearbox gave six forward and two reverse speeds [early models had four forward gears]. Its starting procedure when very cold involved inserting a special cartridge in the cylinder head [which protruded under the radiator] which, when ignited with the piston past the top of its stroke, provided enough heat and momentum to push the massive 8 inch bore piston through its 10½ inch stroke [1931/2 dimensions], turn the flywheel and start the engine

146   Tractors [London] Ltd made Trusty two wheel market garden machines through the 1930's and war years. After the war these were joined by four wheel Trusty Steed ride-on versions. This curious variation photographed in 1953 without its bonnet has an industrial version of a 600cc Norton motorcycle engine. The more conventional Trusty Steed with pneumatic tyres instead of tracks was available with a wide choice of rear and mid mounted implements. Its 4.5hp engine and three forward gears made light two furrow ploughing possible

147 The Fordson Major was produced from 1945 to 1952 and was soon offered with half track and full track conversions. This full track Major by Roadless Traction of Hounslow, photographed ploughing at Wallingford in 1952, is fitted with the Perkins P6 diesel engine which was available optionally to the usual TVO engine

148 After Howard of Rotovator fame sold his interest in Fowler he began to develop his own Platypus crawler tractors. They were originally designed to replace the small Fowlers as special Rotovator machines but were soon offered for more general agricultural purposes. This is a 1952 example and the Jowett Bradford service vans in the background are noteworthy as Jowett had just gone out of business and were about to sell their factory to International Harvester. The Platypus was available until 1958 and started with a choice of petrol or diesel engines, but soon standardised on four cylinder Perkins diesel units of 34 to 51 bhp. Special high-flotation Bogmaster versions were offered with tracks up to 32 inches wide

149 One of the most popular post-war tractors was the Fordson Diesel Major [also available with vaporising oil and petrol engines] which replaced the E27N Major in 1952. The petrol version had an engine capacity of 3261cc whilst the diesel and TVO models were both of 3610cc, the former being rated at 31.4/37.7hp. Six forward and two reverse gears were available. The Major was the basis of a great many conversions to all wheel drive, and half or full track. The County conversion to 4x4 with four equal size wheels and their full track were the most popular and in time County evolved as a make of tractor in its own right. Here a 1955 Diesel Major collects 65 bales on a pallet

150 The Nuffield tractor did not acquire a diesel engine until the fifties. Originally a Perkins P4, the BMC four cylinder was soon substituted, when the tractor was known as the Nuffield Universal DM4. However, petrol [PM4] and vaporising oil [M4] models were still available. The 1957 tractor shown here is the Universal Three, which used a three cylinder version of the 34.5bhp four cylinder BMC diesel. It was a good tractor but never attained the popularity of the little Ford Dexta, or Massey-Ferguson 35, on account of its large size. Following the merger of the British Motor Corporation, of which Morris Motors Ltd Agricultural Division was a part, with Leyland in 1968 the Nuffield range was renamed Leyland in December 1969 and its colour changed from orange to blue

151 This unusual machine is the prototype Roadless crawler exhibited at the Royal Show in 1954. It had a 20hp Perkins diesel and six forward and two reverse gears. Tracks up to three feet wide could be fitted and the machine was aimed particularly at the export market. As it turned out, Roadless Traction's J17 conversion to the Fordson Major showed more promise and was produced instead

152 From its introduction in 1946, when 316 were produced, the Ferguson TE range had achieved 359,092 sales by the time that the company merged with Massey-Harris in August 1953. The Continental engines had been gradually phased out in favour of Standard-built units of 28.5 belt horsepower from 1947 and were all used up by July 1948. The Standard engined versions were called TEA20 and were followed by a vaporising oil version in 1949 [TED20] and a diesel version in 1951 [TEF20] when 12 volt electrics became standard. For a time from 1948 a special TO20 was made in America for use there. It was made partly from British components, at Ferguson Park plant, Detroit, and stayed in production until FE35 [TO35] appeared in '59 but the US TO35 kept the old TE-TO bonnet and radiator styling. In Britain, Perkins offered P3 conversions from 1952 and in 1956 all models were replaced by the grey and gold FE35 shown here with choice of 37bhp Standard petrol or diesel engines or 30bhp V.O. engines. In November 1957 the FE35 became the MF35 and acquired familiar Massey-Ferguson red and grey paintwork. Late in 1957 came the Perkins engined 50.5bhp MF65 and in 1959 Perkins Engines Ltd was acquired by Massey-Ferguson

153 The David Brown 2D of 1956 was an ingenious rethink of traditional tractor/implement ideas. The two cylinder air cooled 12bhp diesel engine was at the rear and there were four forward and one reverse gears. The idea was that whilst the machine could be used for conventional towing, the more precise duties of planting and hoeing would be accomplished directly in front of the driver's eyes, as with this sugar beet drill on its mid-mounted tool bar. The 2D was popular with the larger market gardeners and nurserymen but found little application in larger scale farming. An interesting feature was that its lift was pneumatic and hydraulic and the tubular frame was the air reservoir

154 The McCormick International B-250 which appeared in 1956 was the first International both designed and built in Britain. It had a 2363cc four cylinder 28/30hp diesel engine and a five forward speed gearbox. It was steeped in British vehicle history, being made in the old Jowett works in Bradford and having its crankshaft built by the Maudslay Motor Co. It featured a differential lock and disc brakes and had live hydraulics from a camshaft driven pump

155 With the end of their single cylinder tractors Marshall made one final batch of wheeled machines in 1957-60 before concentrating on Track-Marshalls. Called the MP6 they were powered by six cylinder Leyland 70bhp diesels and had six forward speeds giving up to 13 mph. Britain was not ready for such a large and powerful tractor at the time and of 197 made only ten were sold at home. The rest were sent to all parts of the world, notably to the West Indies for sugar cane cultivation. With water ballasted rear tyres the MP6 had a drawbar pull of almost 10,000 lbs

156 In 1957 David Brown's new 900 diesel tractor appeared. It had a four cylinder 2705cc engine developing 40bhp and six forward and two reverse gears. TVO and petrol engines were also available and in 1957 the Livedrive version appeared with dual clutch giving live hydraulics and live pto. Since 1972 the tractor division of the firm has been owned by Tenneco, the owners of Case. David Brown also had an earlier connection with the USA when they made 2148 tractors for Oliver to sell as their green and white 500 [DB850] and 600 [DB990] in 1960/63

157 Like International, Allis-Chalmers began to assemble tractors in Britain after the Second World War. They began with their popular B model [announced in the USA in 1938] and then introduced the D270 from their Essendine Works near Stamford in 1956. It could have four cylinder 2053cc [like the Model B] petrol or vaporising oil engines or the Perkins P3 2359cc diesel engine. Four forward and one reverse gears were provided. The D270 evolved into the D272 shown here in 1959 with P3 engine but Allis-Chalmers soon discontinued tractor manufacture in Britain and now specialises in larger horsepower tractors and earth-moving machinery in the USA

INDEX OF PHOTOGRAPHS

A.
AGE. 69
Alldays & Onions. 52, 86.
Allis-Chalmers. 80, 100, 103, 122, 125, 131, 157.
Austin. 44, 74.
Avery. 48.

B.
Bates Steel Mule. 26.
Bean. 132.
Benz, Mercedes-Benz. 68.
Beat-em-All. 76.
Blackstone. 43.
Braby. 2.
Bristol. 136.
British Anzani. 102.
Brown, David. 118, 121, 137, 153, 156.
Bull. 19A, 19B.
Byron. 134.

C.
Case. 51, 79, 107, 113.
Caterpillar. 75, 81, 91, 107, 116, 127.
Clayton & Shuttleworth. 11, 45.
Cletrac. 51, 63B, 94, 105.
Cleveland Motor Plow. 18A.
Coney. 8.
Crawley. 48.

D.
Daimler. 13.
Denning. 41.
Dennis. 5.
Deere, John. 31, 62, 65, 111.
Dragon. 133.

E.
Emerson-Brantingham. 38.

F.
Farmall. 73, 92, 109, 114, 141.
Ferguson. 98, 99, 107, 135, 152.
Fiat. 54, 55.
Foden. 77.
Fordson. 23A, 23B, 50, 55, 58, 66, 85, 96, 124, 129, 138, 147, 149.
Fowler. 1, 34, 63A, 64A, 64B, 84, 93A,B,C, 119, 130.

G.
GO. 42.
Galloway. 53A, 53B.
Garner. 53A, 53B, 142.
Garrett. 69.
Glasgow. 33.
Gray. 35.

H.
Heider. 39.
Holt. 6, 14.

I.
Ideal. 10.
Illinois Super Drive. 47.
International [see also Farmall]. 17, 22A, 22B, 24A, 24B, 24C, 28, 50, 59, 61, 87, 89, 104, 108, 120, 126, 154.
Interstate. 27.
Ivel. 3A, 3B.

K.
Kardell. 49.
Killen-Strait. 50.
Koenig St Georges. 15A, 15B.

L.
Lanz. 71.
Latil. 72.
Loyd. 133.

M.
Mann. 21.
Manton. 125.
Marshall. 7, 88, 95, 145, 155.
Martin. 36.
Massey-Harris. 70, 82, 110.
McCormick-Deering - see International.

McLaren. 68.
Minneapolis-Moline. 112, 117, 123.
Moline. 18B.
Moseley. 47.

N.
Nuffield. 139, 150.

O.
Oliver. 83, 101, 106, 115, 128.
OM. 78.
Omnitractor. 56.
Ota. 140.
Overtime - see Deere, John.

P.
Pick. 30.
Platypus. 148.

R.
Ransomes & Rapier. 90.
Ransomes, Simms & Jefferies. 97.
Renault. 55.
Roadless. 147. 151.
Rumely. 9.
Rushton. 67A, 67B.

S.
Samson. 40.
Santler. 37.
Saunderson. 12, 29.
Sherman. 144.
Silent Knight. 56.
Storey. 60.
Straits. 50.

T.
Trusty. 146.
Turner. 143.
Twin City. 57.

W.
Wallis. 16, 25, 46.
Wallis & Steevens. 4.
Walsh & Clark. 20.
Waterloo Boy - see Deere, John.
Weeks-Dungey. 32.
Wyles. 34.

Published by Frederick Warne (Publishers) Ltd, London

© Frederick Warne (Publishers) Ltd

Second Edition 1978
Fourth Impression 1981

ISBN 0 7232 2857 4

Designed by: Brian Harris

Printed by: Butler & Tanner Ltd, Frome and London